MARTIN MODEL 262 *CONVOY FIGHTER*

THE NAVAL VTOL TURBOPROP PROJECT OF 1950

Jared A. Zichek

RETROMECHANIX PRODUCTIONS

First published in the United States of America in 2015 by Jared A. Zichek, 2750 Torrey Pines Rd, La Jolla, California 92037, USA

E-mail: editor@retromechanix.com

©2015 Jared A. Zichek

ISBN: 978-0-9968754-0-0

www.retromechanix.com

All images in this publication are scanned from documents held by National Archives II, College Park, MD, RG 72 unless otherwise indicated. All color profile artwork is ©2015 Jared A. Zichek. Printed in USA.

Front Cover: Contemporary artist's impression of the Martin Model 262 convoy fighter proposal of 1950, one of the unsuccessful rivals to the Convair XFY-1 and Lockheed XFV-1. Below this is a speculative color profile of the same aircraft in the overall Glossy Sea Blue scheme which was standard for most Navy aircraft in this period.

▲ 1

Introduction

In my second book on the US Navy convoy fighter competition of 1950, I present the proposal from the Glenn L. Martin Company of Baltimore, Maryland. Martin was one of five participating contractors, the others being Convair, Goodyear (previously covered), Lockheed, and Northrop. Contracts were eventually awarded in May 1951 to Convair and Lockheed, who built the XFY-1 *Pogo* and XFV-1 *Salmon*, respectively.

The turboprop tailsitter concept emerged in the late 1940s, with the US Navy Bureau of Aeronautics (BuAer) beginning to seriously examine the feasibility of developing a vertical takeoff and landing (VTOL) tailsitter aircraft to protect convoys, task forces, and other vessels. These specialized interceptors would be placed on the decks of ships to provide a rapid defensive and reconnaissance capability

until conventional carrier-based fighters could arrive and assist. The Battle of the Atlantic was fresh in the minds of Navy planners, who were concerned that the Soviets would engage in a similar campaign against merchant shipping if the nascent Cold War erupted into open conflict. BuAer's interest in a VTOL tailsitter fighter coincided with the development of new turboprop engines which provided enough horsepower to make the concept a reality.

BuAer's *Outline Specification for Class VF Airplane (Convoy Fighter) OS-122* was dated July 10, 1950. It listed the requirements for such an aircraft along with a three-quarter scale demonstrator to verify the soundness of the concept. The document was distributed to the major aircraft manufacturers of the day, with the aforementioned companies responding

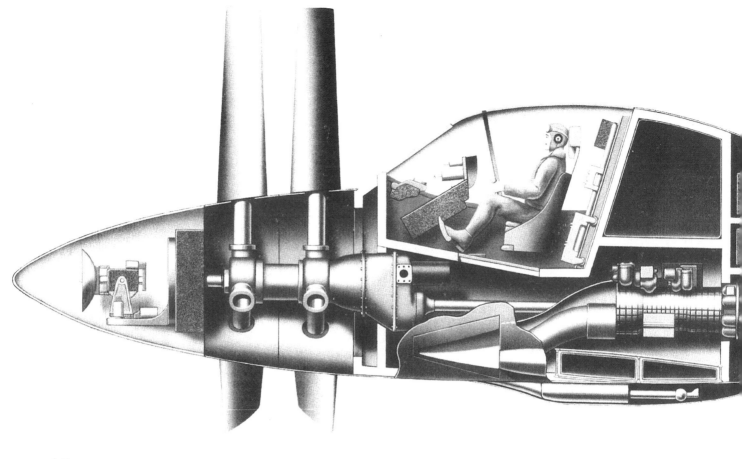

in late November 1950. The products of this competition, the Convair XFY-1 and Lockheed XFV-1, never made it beyond the prototype stage, as they proved to be very difficult to land, suffered from power plant reliability issues, and were eclipsed in performance by contemporary jet fighters. The *Pogo* and *Salmon* became historical curiosities, regularly making the list of world's worst/strangest aircraft; the VTOL turboprop tailsitter configuration proved to be a dead end.

While not as bizarre as the Goodyear GA-28, Martin's Model 262 distinguished itself from the other convoy fighter proposals in that it did not land on its tail; instead, it was designed to land on a vertical platform by means of a retractable nose spike and two small wing gears, hanging from the surface like a mounted insect. This deviation from BuAer's expectations may have been one of several reasons the Model 262 never went beyond the drawing board.

Martin devoted 3½ months of serious engineering effort toward a study of the problems associated with the development of a vertically rising fighter designed to be based on a merchant ship and to supply air defense for the convoy. These studies confirmed the feasibility of developing a convoy fighter that would meet the intent of the requirements set forth for the airplane, leading Martin to the conclusions drawn below.

Martin believed that a large amount of quantita-tive data, which were not available at the time of the competition, needed to be obtained before deciding on an optimum configuration which would ensure success. The required information was basically aerodynamic and was two-fold; first, the effect of a propeller absorbing unusually high horsepower on the horizontal flight characteristics of the airplane, and second, the aerodynamics of the airplane in essentially vertical (hovering) flight. These data could be obtained through a well-planned wind tunnel program.

Martin believed that a satisfactory method for launching and recovering the aircraft from a merchant ship could be developed. The optimum method depended to a great extent on the information obtained during the flight testing of the prototype (scale model) airplane. These tests would supply data on hovering flight characteristics and control response, and permit the development of techniques upon which a sound recovery method could be evolved.

Martin believed that the utilization of this kind of aircraft was not limited to the role of convoy fighter. Its tactical potential in many other phases of naval warfare was tremendous, and Martin was intensely interested in becoming associated with its development.

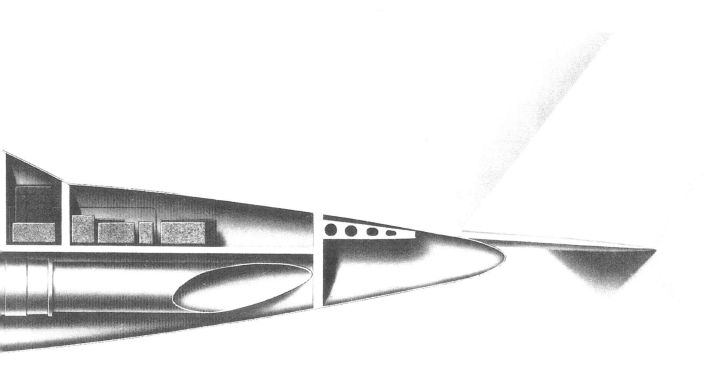

2) A simplified inboard profile of the Martin Model 262 showing the internal layout of this remarkable VTOL turboprop fighter.

General Overview

During the course of preparing the proposal, Martin's primary objective was to develop as complete an understanding of all aspects of the problem as possible. In so doing, many different configurations were investigated. Of all the various possibilities studied, the Model 262 appeared to be the best solution to the problem based on the data available at the time the proposal was submitted.

Certain considerations, however, indicated the desirability of further investigation of modified arrangements. Martin proposed investigating the most promising of these modifications in the wind tunnel to ensure the selection of the optimum aerodynamic arrangement. These modifications are shown later in this book, along with a discussion of their outstanding features.

The basic Martin Model 262 was a swept-wing airplane powered by a 7,500 horsepower XT-40-A-8 turboprop engine driving 16 ft contra-rotating propellers. The development of the gas turbine engine to this equivalent shaft horsepower output made it possible for the airplane to hover by supporting its 16,890 lbs of weight entirely on the thrust of the engine. A suitable device was designed to be mounted on a merchant ship to launch and recover the airplane in its hovering attitude.

The mission of the Model 262 was to protect convoy vessels from enemy air attack. To do this, the airplane was capable of making a transition from the hovering (vertical flight) attitude to a horizontal attitude where it was designed to operate close to sonic speed at attitudes up to 45,000 ft. It carried a single pilot and was equipped with an ejection seat in a pressurized cockpit. Its armament consisted of four 20 mm cannon. Fire control was provided either by a visual computing sight or by use of the radar mounted in the aircraft which was capable of both search and tracking operations. Automatic control devices

PHYSICAL CHARACTERISTICS	
DESIGN WEIGHTS	
TAKE-OFF GROSS WEIGHT	16,890 LBS.
FUEL (500 GALLONS)	3,000 LBS.
COMBAT WEIGHT	15,690 LBS.
LANDING WEIGHT	15,090 LBS.
WEIGHT EMPTY	12,665 LBS.
DIMENSIONS	
SPAN	31.5 FT.
LENGTH	44.7 FT.
HEIGHT	16.0 FT.
WING AREA	247 SQ. FT.
WING ASPECT RATIO	4
SWEEP BACK OF 40% WING CHORD	45°

were provided to assist the pilot. The airplane was designed to be readily adaptable to high rate production with special emphasis on ease of maintenance.

Launch & Recovery

In studying the operation of the convoy fighter from a merchant ship, it became apparent that the problems involved in launching the aircraft were far less complex than those encountered in recovery. Martin's efforts were therefore directed toward solving the recovery problem. The method which Martin evolved permitted launching the aircraft from the same equipment that was used for the recovery.

---

3) The key performance figures of the Martin Model 262 along with a diagram of its principle mission.

Note: Explanations for the illustrations shown on the next several pages are located in the main text immediately adjacent.

Recovery. The feasibility of any recovery method depended primarily on the degree of control that the pilot had over the airplane in hovering flight. If it was assumed that he had perfect control with instantaneous response, it was possible to land the airplane on its tail on a platform area with little or no auxiliary equipment on the surface ship. If it was assumed that pilot control and response rate were poor, recovery methods involving elaborate deck equipment were required. Martin's proposed recovery method was about midway between these two extremes. The company believed that proof of the ultimate method depended on flight tests and techniques that would be developed on the prototype.

The landing area was defined by specification as being 200 ft aft and 25 ft above the pitch and roll center of the ship. The specification also required that a landing be made while the ship was rolling at ±15° and pitching ±4°. This pitch and roll induced a total vertical motion of the landing area of 28 ft and a sideways motion of 13 ft. Martin's recommend-

MAXIMUM SPEED. . . . . 540 KNOTS
    AT 35,000 FT., COMBAT WEIGHT, MILITARY POWER

COMBAT CEILING. . . . . 47,570 FT
    AT COMBAT WEIGHT, MILITARY POWER

TIME TO CLIMB TO 35,000 FT. . . . . 5.2 MIN
    FROM STANDSTILL, MILITARY POWER

ENDURANCE (LOITER TIME) . . . . 115 MIN
    SEE COMBAT PROBLEM BELOW

MANEUVERABILITY 4.8
    MAXIMUM LOAD FACTOR AT 35,000 FT., COMBAT WEIGHT, AT MAXIMUM SPEED

COMBAT 3 MIN.   35000 FT.   LOITER TIME
MILITARY POWER

COMBAT PROBLEM

LANDING 5 MIN.   TAKE-OFF 5 MIN.
MILITARY POWER   MILITARY POWER

▲ 3

← 100 N. MILES →

ed recovery method could be accomplished in the specified landing area or in an area immediately aft of amid-ships adjacent to the No. 4 hatch. This latter location was recommended since it was only 80 ft aft of the center of rotation in pitch where the vertical motion induced by pitch was only about 11 ft.

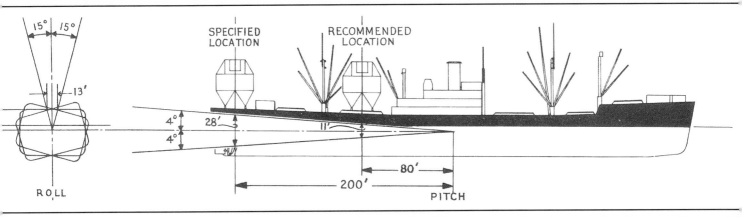

Equipment on Surface Ship.

A platform was mounted vertically at the landing area of the ship. This platform was hinged about a fore and aft axis and was power operated through a rack and pinion. It was stabilized in such a manner that no sideways motion was imparted to the point "A" by roll of the ship.

The point "A" was in the center of a contact area approximately 10 ft on a side. The contact area consisted of a series of vee-shaped welded steel members which extended from the top to the bottom of the area. A series of shock absorbing arresting cables were stretched horizontally across and behind these vertical members. The remainder of the platform

EQUIPMENT ON SURFACE SHIP

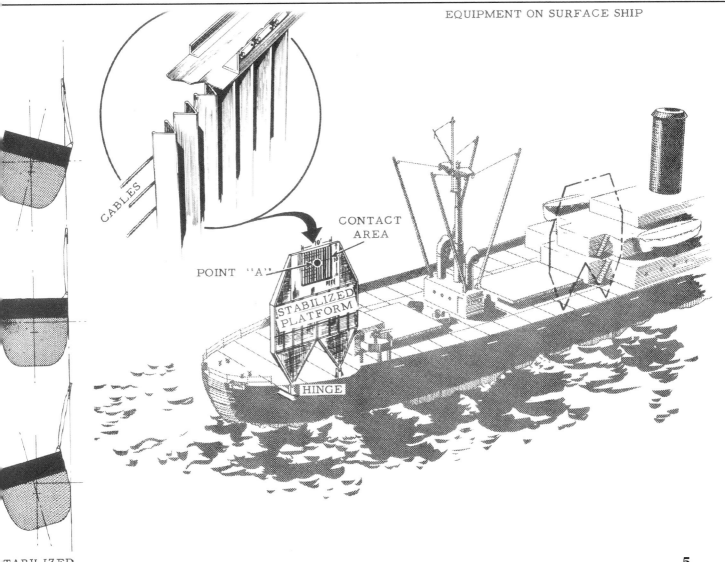

was covered with light steel grating with a reinforced region below the contact area. A protected station for a landing signal officer was situated on top of the platform.

A retractable spike was located just aft of the propeller plane and two retractable wing gears were located on each wing panel. The spike consisted of a short stroke shock absorbing unit with a pointed end equipped with a spring loaded latch which locked the spike in the contact area of the platform when it was pushed through the opening between the vertical vee-shaped members on the platform.

The pilot's seat was rotated through 45° when in the hovering attitude to place the pilot in a comfortable position for the vertical flight attitude and enable him to look down and over the sides of the airplane. A window in the floor of the airplane permitted him to see the end of the spike directly for final alignment prior to contact.

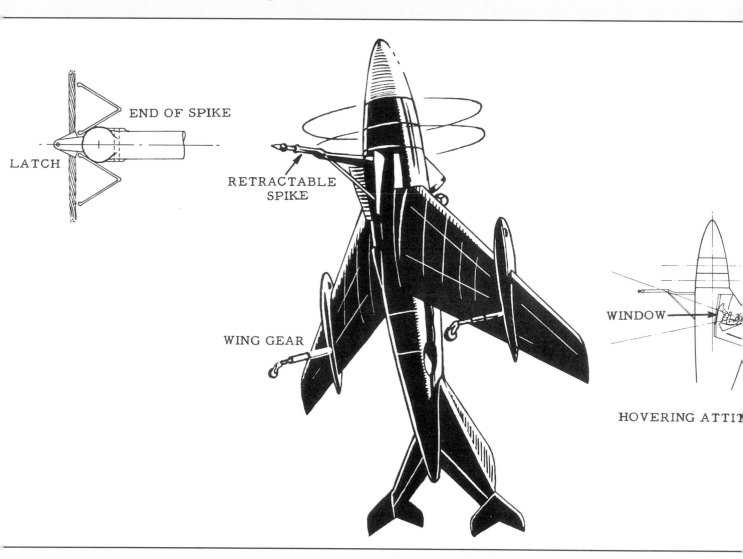

END OF SPIKE

LATCH

RETRACTABLE SPIKE

WING GEAR

WINDOW

HOVERING ATTIT

Recovery Method. The landing was accomplished after making a transition from the horizontal to the vertical flight attitude, by an approach from aft of the ship with the wings approximately aligned with the fore and aft axis of the surface ship. Under these conditions, the pilot's view of the ship was ideal since the ship was out to the side and slightly below the airplane.

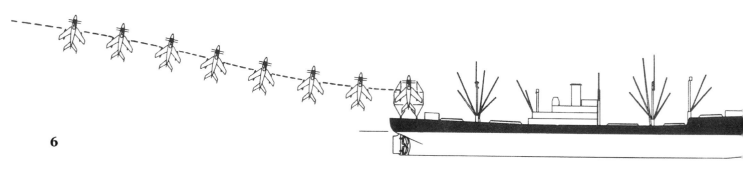

The pilot maneuvered the airplane to a position just outboard of the landing platform. Since the platform was stabilized so as to transcribe no lateral motion to the point "A" due to roll of the ship, and since the ship's speed was constant, the only significant motion of the platform relative to the airplane was essentially along the vertical axis of the airplane and was induced by pitching of the ship.

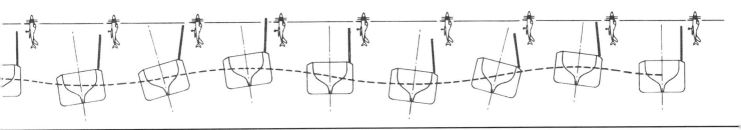

With this situation, the pilot was able to maintain a position prior to contact such that the spike was just outboard of the platform. Under normal sea conditions when the pilot was ready to make contact, he would pitch the airplane gently toward the platform, so as to fly the airplane toward the platform. The spike could strike the platform anywhere in the 10 ft by 10 ft contact area. The vee-shaped vertical members guided the spike into the slot between the members. When the spike had fully penetrated the slot, a spring loaded latch locked it in the slot and sent a signal which either cut the power automatically or told the pilot to do so. During heavy seas, the pilot would hover at constant altitude just outboard of the platform until he could anticipate the relative vertical motion of the platform. With the assistance of the signal officer, he would engage the contact area as the ship came up to meet him near the top of its vertical motion.

If the spike missed the contact area and struck the grating around it, it would tilt the airplane's nose away from the platform, since the spike was above the airplane center of gravity. This would cause the airplane to move away from the platform and permitted a second approach.

With the power cut and the spike engaged, the airplane was allowed to move down the platform about 3 ft as its vertical motion was reduced to zero by one of the horizontal arresting cables that was engaged by the spike. During this motion the wing gears contacted the platform, and the recovery was complete.

The platform was then rotated down to a horizontal position and the airplane was re-positioned for takeoff and secured.

Launch. To position the airplane for takeoff, the arresting cables were relaxed and the airplane was maneuvered so as to slide the spike to the top of the slot where it engaged a quick-release mechanism.

 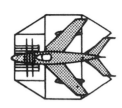 

QUICK RELEASE

The pilot entered the airplane, checked it out, and started the engines while the platform was in the horizontal position. Just prior to takeoff, the platform was rotated to its vertical stabilized position. As power was applied, the airplane raised off the wing gears, the spike was released from the quick release mechanism by the pilot or signal officer, and the airplane left the platform.

When takeoff or recovery was made with the relative wind coming in from the side of the ship, the platform would be stabilized in a position slightly off the vertical in order to match the hovering attitude of the airplane.

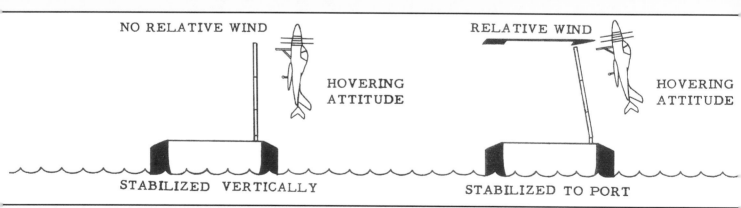

NO RELATIVE WIND

HOVERING ATTITUDE

STABILIZED VERTICALLY

RELATIVE WIND

HOVERING ATTITUDE

STABILIZED TO PORT

To permit the airplane to be rolled around on the deck or dock areas, the spike was designed to accommodate a small wheel and jack assembly. When attached to the spike, this assembly permitted the airplane to be jacked up to support the weight on the wheel.

8

For training and shore based operations, the platform could be mounted on a trailer which served as its takeoff and recovery vehicle as well as for ground handling.

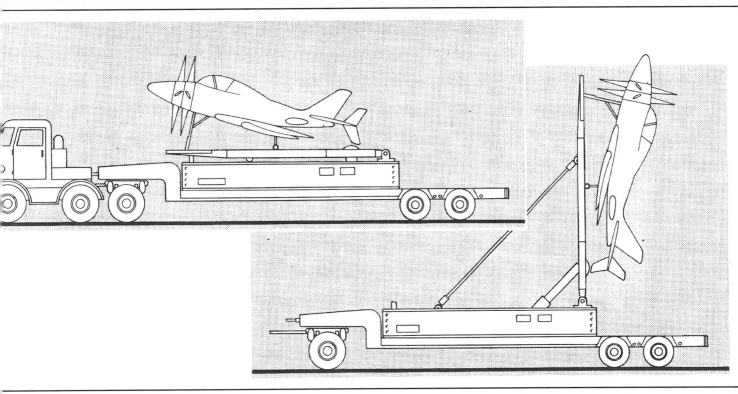

▼ 4

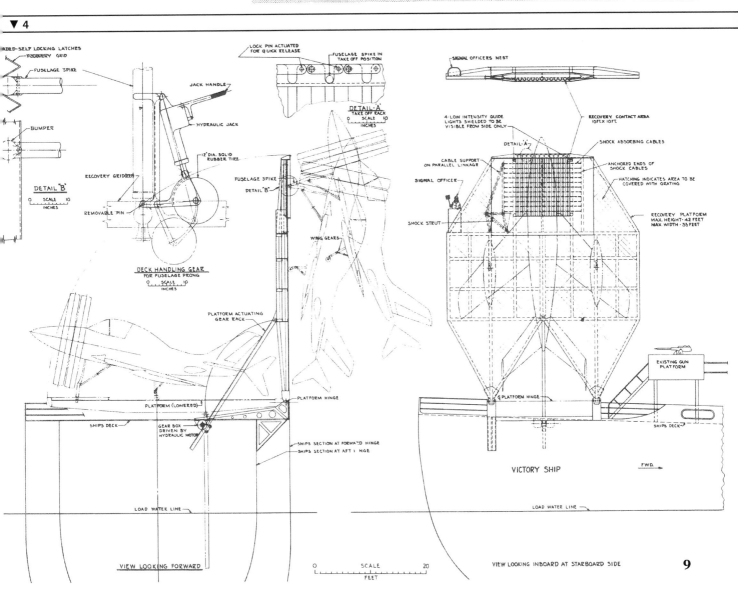

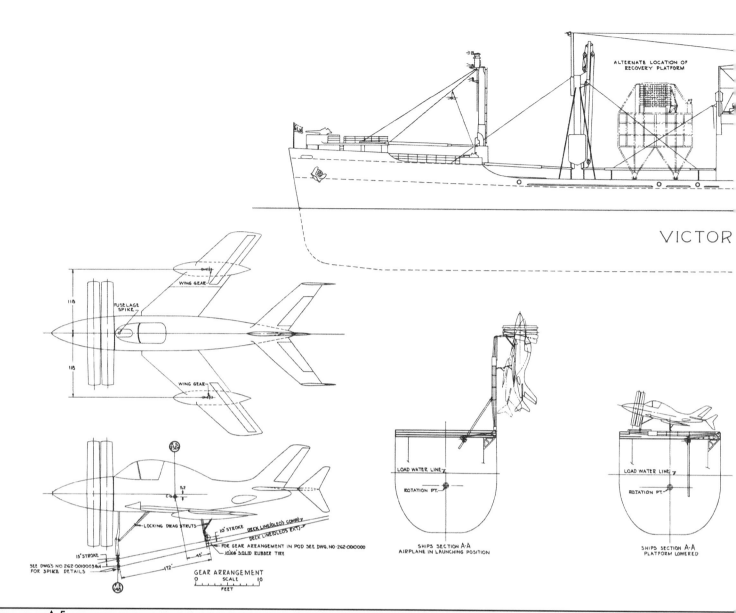

VICTOR

GEAR ARRANGEMENT
SCALE
FEET

SHIPS SECTION A-A
AIRPLANE IN LAUNCHING POSITION

SHIPS SECTION A-A
PLATFORM LOWERED

▲ 5

Previous Page:
4) Detailed schematic of the hinged recovery platform mounted on a merchant vessel with the Martin Model 262 attached.

This Spread:
5) General arrangement of the Model 262's launch and recovery system showing various possible locations of the recovery platform on a Liberty Ship as well as how the platform could be adjusted to the rolling motion of the ship in rough seas.

Martin believed that this recovery method could be developed to fulfill the intended purpose, though additional thought and analysis was required. One contemplated refinement was to study the means of providing shock absorption in the platform that was more than just the vertical direction as provided by the horizontal arresting cables. If this were done, the shock absorbing units in the spike and wing gears on the airplane could have been shortened to reduce the alighting gear weight carried in the airplane.

Aerodynamics

During the preparation of the convoy fighter proposal, major emphasis was placed on the recognition of the aerodynamic problems involved and on studies of the many solutions to these problems. The mission of this airplane was such that it was extremely important to have an exceptionally sound basic aerodynamic design. The attainment of the optimum tactical configuration required a considerable amount of basic analytical aerodynamic studies, wind tunnel tests, and eventually flight tests of a prototype to solve those problems not previously encountered on an aircraft. While it was feasible to design a vertically rising aircraft which was also capable of obtaining speeds approaching that of sound, a complete understanding of the various problems associated with this airplane was necessary at the onset if the design was to proceed on a sound basis.

Since the most critical feature of the airplane concerned its flying qualities, primary emphasis was

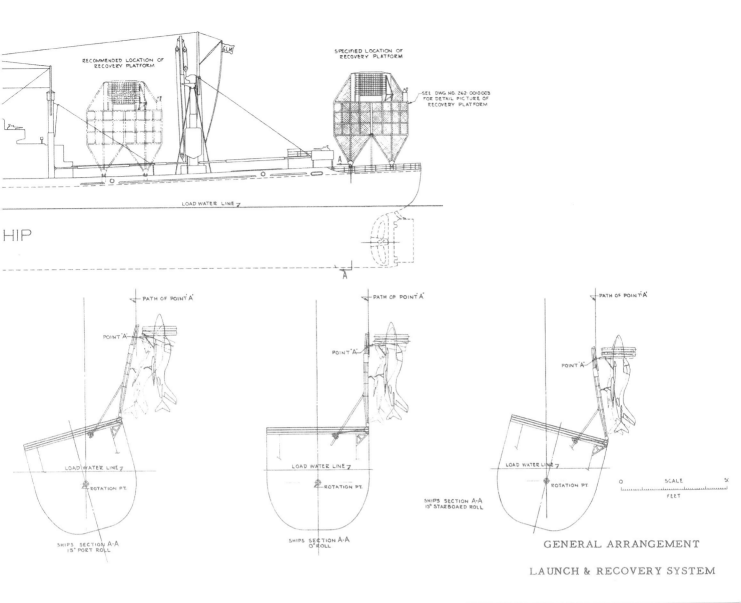

GENERAL ARRANGEMENT

LAUNCH & RECOVERY SYSTEM

placed on the stability and control characteristics of the airplane in hovering, transition, and in level flight attitudes. A summary of the more important aerodynamic considerations followed.

One means of obtaining the desired stability characteristics during some or all modes of flight was through the use of automatic electronic and mechanical devices. It did not appear advisable during the preliminary design stages to base a configuration entirely upon the use of automatic stabilization. Consequently, Martin's approach was to develop a configuration which was inherently stable aerodynamically and not to rely on the use of synthetic stabilizing devices. These devices could have been used, but they would not have been employed to refine the stability characteristics of the airplane and would not have been used in lieu of good aerodynamic design.

Hovering. During hovering, it was desirable to have the airplane tend to maintain a vertical attitude even in gusty air. To accomplish this, it was neces-sary that the airplane not tend to weather-cock (turn) into the relative wind. If the airplane had a large tail, a horizontal gust would rotate the airplane into the relative wind. The airplane would then begin to translate, tending to fly into the gust. The increase in relative wing wind would further rotate the airplane into the gust. It was clear that the motion was divergent.

With a smaller tail, it was possible to make the airplane neutrally stable during hovering. In this case the airplane would not tend to rotate, but would only translate when subjected to a horizontal gust. After the gust subsided, the translation would also subside.

Thus, during hovering, no strong tendency to weather-cock into the wind was tolerated. However, in the normal level flight attitude, it was necessary that the airplane weather-cock into the relative wind if the airplane were to be stable. Martin therefore concluded that a large tail effect was desired during level flight while a small tail effect was desired during hovering.

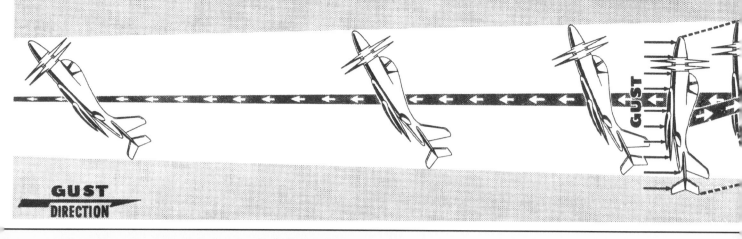

For longitudinal stability, two effects could be used to make the hovering and level flight characteristics compatible. These were:

1. The downwash behind the wing was much greater during hovering than in level flight. This resulted in a desirable decrease in the stabilizing contribution of the horizontal tail.

2. With a sweptback wing and the propeller in front of the wing, the slipstream acted only over the central portion during hovering. Since the wing was swept back, the center of lift moved forward relative to its position in level flight. The result was a desired decrease in the tendency to weather-cock into the wind during hovering.

Actually, the above two aerodynamic effects may have been too great and resulted in an undesirably large tendency to weather-cock away from the wind during hovering. Wind tunnel tests were required to determine the proper balance.

In the directional case the above two aerodynamic effects did not exist and special consideration had to be given to the vertical tail design. It appeared very possible to make the level flight and hovering directional characteristics compatible by locating a portion of the vertical tail outside the slipstream. This was accomplished by the use of three vertical tails, one centrally located with the other two on the edge of the slipstream. Thus, in hovering, only the central vertical tail was effective while in level flight the entire tail was effective. If wind tunnel tests showed that large gusts caused the slipstream to drift over the leeward fin to an appreciable extent, it was possible to eliminate the contribution of this fin by the use of outwardly deflected tip rudders. This prevented the leeward fin from contributing to the tendency to weather-cock into the wing. These tip rudders, if required, would be deflected to a given position only during hovering.

During hovering, the control surfaces had to be located in the slipstream. The lateral control was seriously handicapped by this requirement since it was

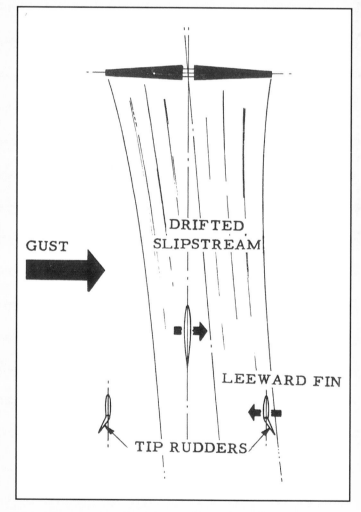

not possible to obtain a large moment arm. Thus, if inboard wing ailerons were used exclusively, it would have been necessary for them to develop large changes in lift. If the aileron were designed to produce the large changes in lift, however, it was expected that the resulting change in downwash at the tail would have tended to give a rolling moment opposing that of the ailerons.

While some available data indicated that the reversing effect of the tail did not exist, at least when the inboard ailerons produced a small rolling moment, it did not appear reasonable to ignore this possibility since other test data showed that the tail

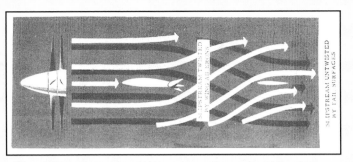

roll reversal effect did exist. Therefore, the latest control had been located on the tail. It was expected that the elevator, operated differentially, would have produced adequate roll control during hovering. While the amount of control possible with the tail elevons may have been limited, the magnitude of the required roll control was not expected to be large. If future studies and tests showed that the proposed lateral control was marginal, some additional control could have been achieved by the use of inboard ailerons in conjunction with the tail elevons. Another possibility was the use of differentially operated all-movable tails.

Transition. The transition maneuver involved the change from vertical to horizontal flight attitude in takeoff and from horizontal to vertical in landing. A "zoom" type transition involving a change in altitude in which the angle of attack was kept below the stall for the entire wing, or a level flight transition with no significant change in altitude, were the alternatives. Martin believed that the design philosophy should be directed toward the attainment of an airplane potentially capable of performing level flight transitions. Such an airplane could be capable of level flight at any speed from high speed down to zero speed and was superior to one that had to be maneuvered in a predetermined fashion through a given range of speeds. If an airplane was capable of making level flight transitions it was also capable of making zoom transitions. Martin noted that the airplane had to be capable of level flight in the hovering attitude at least up to speeds of 35 knots even though zoom transition was used. This was necessary in landing when the surface ship was heading into a strong head wind.

The design problem of making an airplane capable of level flight transition was more complicated since the angle of attack became large. The portion of the wing outside the slipstream would have been stalled during a level flight transition. No serious drag or stability complications were anticipated due to this fact. The primary effect would have been a possible buffeting of the airplane. Martin believed that this would not have been a serious disadvantage

due to the low speeds involved. If necessary, several methods existed which could have been used to alleviate this condition. One method was the use of slats to keep the wing tips unstalled at least down to speeds where the aerodynamic forces became negligible. Another method consisted of varying the incidence of the wing tip. A third possibility was the use of a low aspect ratio delta wing which would have had only a negligible portion of the wing stalled.

An analysis of the airplane characteristics during a level flight transition was made for the proposed configuration including the effect of stalled wing tips. The angle of attack of the center portion was below the angle of stall at all speeds due to the action of the slipstream, a desirable but not necessarily a required condition. Although a reversal in the elevator position existed over a portion of the speed range, ample control was available. Wind tunnel tests might have shown that this elevator reversal could be eliminated by the use of wing and tail incidence in conjunction with propeller thrust moment.

In summary, it appeared that it was possible to perform the transition in essentially level flight. It followed that it was possible to perform zoom transitions, since the additional power required was not as high as that required for takeoff.

Level Flight. The primary source of the aerodynamic problems in level flight for this airplane stemmed from the use of the propeller as the propulsive element. The power loading was much higher than normal and the usual power effects were greatly aggravated. This indicated that the propeller design had to be carried out to minimize the very large influence of the propeller on the trim and stability characteristics of the airplane, in addition to obtaining the highest possible propeller efficiencies.

Two propeller design philosophies were considered. In the first, an essentially transonic propeller design was used. The propeller tip Mach number was maintained at approximately unity. This required a low propeller RPM, which in turn resulted in high blade angles. Two serious design problems resulted:

1. A gear-shifting mechanism was required to obtain the low RPM for high speeds and the required high RPM for takeoff and hovering.
2. The large size force developed by such a propeller caused a very serious stability problem. The effect on stability was similar to having a surface of approximately one-third the wing area located at the propeller position.

The above two problems were greatly alleviated by utilizing a supersonic propeller design philosophy.

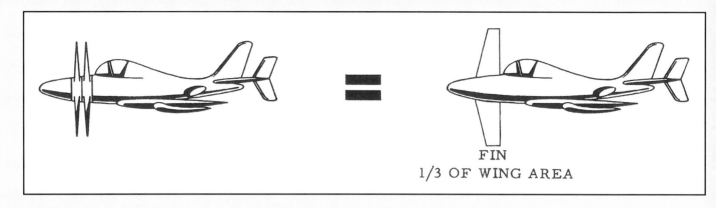

FIN
1/3 OF WING AREA

Most aerodynamic phenomena became critical at Mach 1, whereas improved flow condition existed at supersonic speeds. Therefore, it appeared desirable to design a propeller with a large portion of its blade operating above the speed of sound. To obtain this condition, it was necessary to increase the propeller RPM, making it feasible to eliminate the gear-shifting mechanism. The blade angle, of course, would have been reversed and it then became possible to solve the stability problem in a reasonable manner. Available test data indicated that the efficiency of a supersonic propeller was expected to equal that of the transonic propeller in the high speed range of this airplane.

Since the propeller fin effect was roughly proportional to the number of blades, a six-bladed propeller was preferred to an eight-bladed propeller. The changes in performance were not significant. The figure below shows the relation between the propeller side force with Mach number for the various propellers discussed. Martin strongly recommended a single speed gear box driving a six-bladed supersonic propeller.

A new method was derived to obtain these relations since existing methods did not adequately cover compressibility effects. The derivation of the method was given in G.L.M. Engineering Report 4105, "Considerations of the Dominating Propeller Interference Effects for a Convoy Fighter Design" by H. Multhopp, Nov. 16, 1950.

Even with a six-bladed supersonic propeller having minimum fin effect, relatively large tail sizes were required. This condition could be greatly relieved by locating the propeller in the center portion of the fuselage near the center of gravity of the airplane. A reduced frontal area, and improved visibility would have also been obtained with this arrangement. This required a propeller gearing arrangement which accommodated the structure necessary to connect the fore and aft portions of the fuselage.

In addition to the problem imposed by the propeller, the usual compressibility problems existed on this airplane. High speed rolling effectiveness, usually restricted by aeroelastic influences, was maintained in Martin's design by the use of spoiler ailerons which had but a fraction of the aerodynamic twisting moments of normal ailerons. This proposed lateral control for horizontal flight with its artificial feel had been used successfully at high speeds on the Martin XB-51. Use of a large amount of sweep and a thin airfoil section minimized the adverse effects of compressibility at transonic speeds. A low wing position was used to reduce the possibility of tail buffet at high speed. The low wing allowed a tail location above the wing and still within the slipstream during hovering.

To summarize, the mission of this airplane introduced design considerations not previously encountered. The time available for the preparation of this proposal had been expended in attempting to ascertain the nature of the basic problems and investigate possible forms of solution. The results of the study indicated that although analytical and wind-tunnel work was necessary, Martin was convinced that it was entirely feasible to develop a configuration which would perform the mission desired.

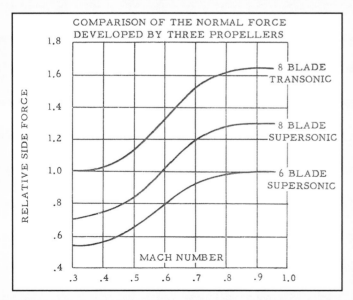

Controls

Surface Controls and Boost. The surface control systems were in general of conventional design. Directional control was provided by foot-operated rudders with no power boost. Longitudinal control was provided by power-boosted elevators. The power boost was designed to cause the pilot to furnish a portion of the force which operated the control surface, thereby supplying aerodynamic feel and enabling him to control the pitch of the airplane in limited maneuvers with the boost system inoperative. Lateral control was provided by differential movements of the elevators and by operation of wing spoilers. The lateral control surfaces were hydraulically operated and mechanically synchronized with the pilot's control, enabling him to operate the surfaces manually in the event of hydraulic failure.

Autopilot. Components of a conventional autopilot such as the Sperry E-4 were used with special sensing equipment to provide the freedom necessary for this aircraft. The servo system of the autopilot was used without modification. Trim servos were provided to keep the airplane control surfaces operating at zero hinge moment during autopilot control to prevent violent aircraft maneuvers and sudden application of forces to the pilot's controls in the event of autopilot failure. A throttle servo was used to control thrust and to complete the set of autopilot functions necessary to provide for all modes of aircraft flight.

A formation stick type of autopilot hand control was located on the pilot's console. Use of this type of control permitted a pilot to maneuver the airplane through the autopilot if he so desired. In the event of power boost failure, the pilot could have combined his own efforts with those of the autopilot to control the airplane.

Automatic Control. The airplane was held stabilized in any attitude of horizontal or vertical flight by the autopilot. Automatic transition from vertical to horizontal flight was provided by programming the airplane's ascent by means of autopilot. A controlled torque was applied to one axis of the autopilot's gyros which caused the gyros to process and operate the airplane's control servos for the transition. During transitional flight the power setting of the engine was changed by the throttle servo to give the proper power setting for each pitch angle.

Automatic transition from horizontal to vertical flight was provided as the reverse of the transition from vertical to horizontal flight. Another method of providing a transition from horizontal flight for use during a blind landing is discussed on the next page.

Artificial roll stability was probably required for the airplane when it was in the vertical attitude. The stability signals obtained from a rate gyro operated the lateral control servo.

The contemporary trend in fire control development was toward fully automatic flight control of the airplane during the attack phase of the mission. The basic components required to do this, that is the tracking radar, computer and autopilot, were installed in the airplane. Martin gave definite consideration to completely automatic attack during the development of the control system for the airplane.

Electronics Installation. The electronics equipment installed in the aircraft included:

1. AN/ARC-27—UHF Transmitter-Receiver
2. AN/ARR-2A—Navigation Unit
3. AN/APN-22—Radio Altimeter
4. AN/APX-6—IFF Unit

In addition, the aircraft carried an AN/APQ-42 radar and a small beacon furnished by Martin for use in blind landing.

In conformance with OS-122, both the AN/APG-25 and the AN/APS-25 radars were considered. The AN/APG-25 was a 50 kilowatt, monopulse, automatic tracking radar. It had no provisions for search and, owing to the relatively small amount of transmitted power, this radar could not provide adequate search range. For these reasons it was not recommended for use in this application.

The AN/APS-25 was a 250 kilowatt radar which provided for search, acquisition and automatic tracking. For automatic tracking, this radar employed the conical scanning technique. It was well known that radars employing this technique provided a lower degree of tracking accuracy against targets traveling at high angular rates than monopulse radars. Since the AN/APQ-42 provided the same features as the AN/APS-25 but employed the monopulse technique for automatic tracking, this radar was recommended for use in the convoy fighter. Nevertheless, the airframe was capable of accommodating either the AN/APS-25 or the AN/APQ-42 radars.

The arrangement of the radar equipment is shown in the accompanying drawing. It was considered essential that the RF head, which contained the transmitter, be mounted directly behind the scanner in order to obtain the maximum available search range. If the RF head were mounted back in the fuselage, approximately 15 ft of waveguide leading through the propeller shaft to the scanner would have been required. This resulted in a search range

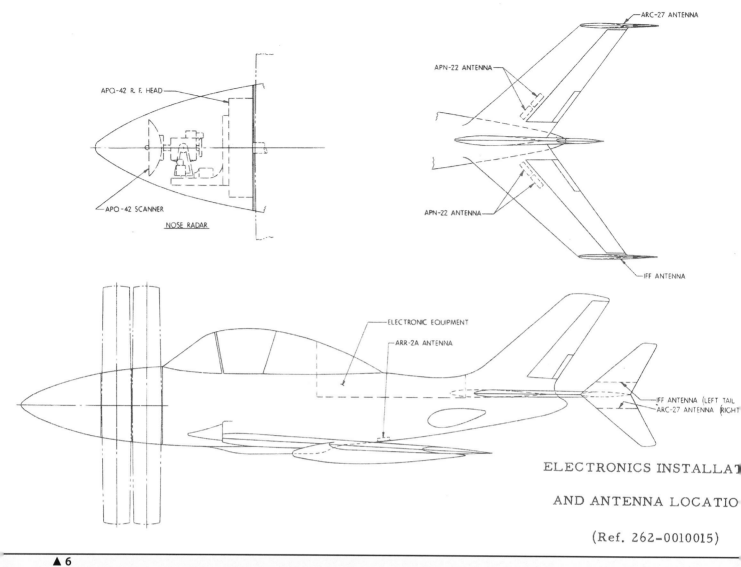

APQ-42 R.F. HEAD

APQ-42 SCANNER

NOSE RADAR

ARC-27 ANTENNA

APN-22 ANTENNA

APN-22 ANTENNA

IFF ANTENNA

ELECTRONIC EQUIPMENT

ARR-2A ANTENNA

IFF ANTENNA (LEFT TAIL
ARC-27 ANTENNA (RIGHT

ELECTRONICS INSTALLAT

AND ANTENNA LOCATIO

(Ref. 262-0010015)

▲ 6

penalty of approximately ten percent. The RF head was consequently mounted in the spinner. It was re-packaged to fit into the 10" depth behind the scanner; this was the only unit of the AN/APQ-42 requiring repackaging.

Blind Landing (Electronics). A fully auto-matic or pilot controlled blind landing system was developed to make the convoy fighter an operable weapon during times of poor visibility. The only basic equipment required in addition to that already employed, the system consisted of a small radar on a surface ship and an airborne beacon, weighing less than 30 lbs, in an aircraft. The system provided the pilot or automatic control devices with all the neces-sary information to bring the aircraft through tran-sition from horizontal to vertical flight which termi-nated directly above the ship, oriented the aircraft's wings parallel to the longitudinal axis of the ship, and executed a descent to the recovery devices on the deck of the ship.

To execute a blind or automatic landing, the pilot turned on his airborne beacon when he was in horizontal flight and his range was about 8 miles

6) Diagram showing the location of the antennas and radar on the Model 262; the electronic equipment was located primarily in the upper mid-fuselage.

from his ship. When the range decreased to 5 miles the shipborne radar detected the beacon and began to automatically track it in angle and in range. The ship's heading angle with respect to magnetic north (obtained from the ship's compass) was added to the azimuth angle of the radar sight line measured with respect to the longitudinal axis of the ship. The resultant angular information was shifted through 90° to provide an azimuth angle, with respect to magnetic north, which represented a perpendicular to the radar sight line. This information was sent to the aircraft, via conventional radio link, where it was compared with the angle between the wing line and magnetic north. The resultant difference, which rep-resented the misalignment of the aircraft wings with the perpendicular to the radar sight line, was used to rotate a line on the face of a 3" cathode ray tube or to feed the automatic control devices which controlled the wing alignment of the aircraft. In this manner, it was possible to maintain the orientation of the aircraft wings perpendicular to the radar sight line and the transition from horizontal to vertical flight could be controlled by means of pitch signals.

The pitch signals were obtained in the following manner. A synthetic elevation angle was generated by means of a motor-driven synchro. This angle was made to increase with time in accordance with the variation in elevation angle which occurred for a representative transition terminating with the aircraft hovering in a vertical attitude directly above the ship. The elevation angle of the sight line was compared with the synthetic angle and the resultant difference signal was transmitted to the aircraft. This signal, which represented a change in speed necessary to bring the aircraft on to the representative transition, was used to displace the line vertically on the face of the indicator or to feed the automatic devices which controlled the pitch and therefore the speed of the aircraft. This technique made possible a completely controlled transition terminating with the aircraft directly above the ship. The throttle servo was con-trolled by signals sensitive to the pitch of the airplane such that the power supplied was that required for horizontal flight at each pitch angle of the airplane. The use of this technique did not restrict the pilot to make the transition in any fashion he desired and the presentation on the cathode ray tube continuously indicated that a change in pitch or wing alignment was necessary to bring the aircraft on to the representative transition selected.

As the sight line approached the vertical, the wing orientation information transmitted from the ship to the aircraft was changed so that when compared with the wing-line angle in the aircraft, the resultant error signal provided the rotation of the line on the indicator necessary to bring the aircraft wings parallel to the longitudinal axis of this ship. At this

7) Illustration of the Model 262's blind landing system in operation; the system would have used an airborne beacon to help accomplish these hazardous recoveries.

▼ 7

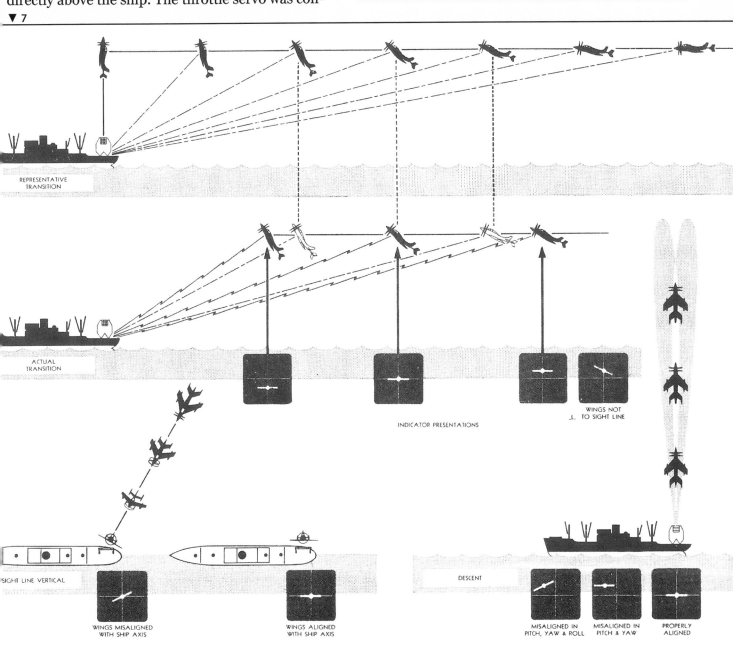

REPRESENTATIVE TRANSITION

ACTUAL TRANSITION

INDICATOR PRESENTATIONS

WINGS NOT ⊥ TO SIGHT LINE

DESCENT

SIGHT LINE VERTICAL

WINGS MISALIGNED WITH SHIP AXIS

WINGS ALIGNED WITH SHIP AXIS

MISALIGNED IN PITCH, YAW & ROLL

MISALIGNED IN PITCH & YAW

PROPERLY ALIGNED

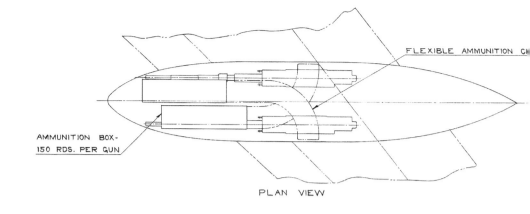

FLEXIBLE AMMUNITION C

AMMUNITION BOX-
150 RDS. PER GUN

PLAN VIEW

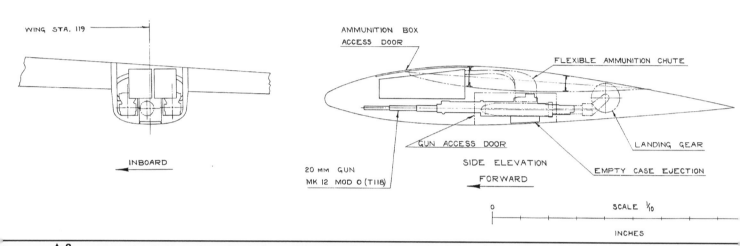

WING STA. 119

INBOARD

AMMUNITION BOX
ACCESS DOOR

FLEXIBLE AMMUNITION CHUTE

GUN ACCESS DOOR

20 MM GUN
MK 12 MOD 0 (T118)

SIDE ELEVATION
FORWARD

LANDING GEAR

EMPTY CASE EJECTION

SCALE 1/10

0

INCHES

▲ 8

point an additional signal representing the position of the sight line measured about the transverse axis of the ship was also sent to the aircraft and was used to deflect the line on the indicator horizontally or to feed automatic devices which controlled the aircraft in yaw. In this manner it was possible for the aircraft to be retained along a vertical line to the deck of the ship and for the wing line to be maintained parallel to the ship's longitudinal axis. Then, by the use of the radar range (height) information, the throttle could be controlled manually or automatically to permit descent to the landing platform of the ship. Since the pilot had to see the landing platform only during the very last part of the recovery, this method permitted recovery during conditions of visibility down to about 75 ft.

Armament

Two 20 mm cannons were mounted adjacent to each of the wing gears in underslung streamlined bodies just outside of the propeller disk. Ammunition was carried in compact boxes in the forward part of the body and loaded through doors on the top.

The fire control system consisted of the recommended AN/APQ-42 radar and the Aero X1A

8) The basic armament of the Model 262 consisted of four 20 mm cannons, two in each underslung wing pod.

computer. A Mark 6, Mod. 1 visual sight unit was also provided. Since the airplane was equipped with automatic flight control devices, consideration was given to the problem of automatically controlling the aircraft during the attack phase. Developments at the MIT Instrument Laboratory had successfully demonstrated the ability of a radar, computer, autopilot combination to control an airplane on an attack course. Westinghouse was also developing a similar system. Preliminary study had shown that the basic Westinghouse control scheme could be applied to this aircraft. The same components of the autopilot system used for the takeoff and landing phase could be utilized for automatic control during the attack phase if the entire system was properly integrated. Future developments in the art of automatic flight control might have produced a system which could maneuver an attacking aircraft to a higher degree of accuracy than could a well trained pilot. Martin recommended that the aircraft control system be designed in such a manner that automatic flight control during the attack phase could be incorporated.

The company also recommended that definite

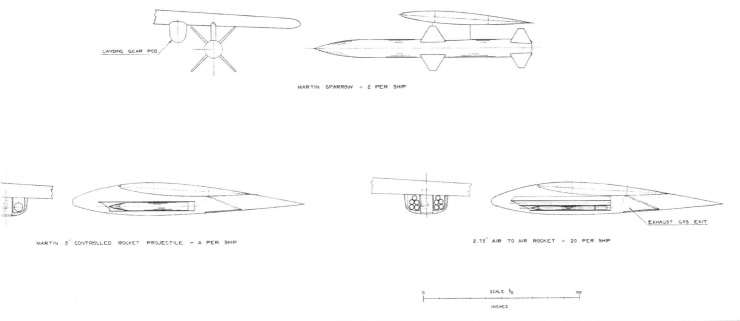

LANDING GEAR POD

MARTIN SPARROW – 2 PER SHIP

MARTIN 5" CONTROLLED ROCKET PROJECTILE – 4 PER SHIP

2.75" AIR TO AIR ROCKET – 20 PER SHIP

EXHAUST GAS EXIT

SCALE ⅒

INCHES

▲ 9

consideration be given during the development of the aircraft and its systems to the use of other weapons such as rockets, either controlled or otherwise, and to the installation of air-to-air missiles.

Power Plant

The engine used was an Allison XT-40-A-8 mounted in the fuselage. The engine reduction gear housing was mounted in the fuselage by means of vibration isolating (dynafocal) mounts which isolated propeller vibration from the power sections and aircraft structure. The dual power unit utilized a three-point mounting arrangement. The two upper mounting pads on the diffuser assembly were used together with the bottom compressor air inlet tie bracket.

The induction system employed separate air intakes located in the fillets between the wing and the fuselage and partly submerged in the fuselage. A revolving door which was designed to impose a minimum amount of drag on the airplane was incorporated in each intake to provide for single power unit operation. A boundary layer bleed was incorporated in the intake to remove boundary air. An almost identical air intake and door were used on the Martin XB-51 and the ram recovery was excellent. Provisions were made in the inlet ducts for passage of the drive shaft housing through the ducts.

The fuel system consisted of a service tank and five auxiliary tanks with a total capacity of 500 gallons of fuel. A constant fuel level was maintained in the service tank by means of constant level valve which controlled the fuel flow from the auxiliary tanks. The service tank was designed so that fuel would be continuously available to the engine at any possible sustained flight attitude by the use of two booster pumps located in opposite ends of the tank

9) Martin also proposed these alternate missile and rocket installations for the Model 262.

and two check valves to prevent the fuel from being pumped back into the tank. The pilot could direct fuel to either or both power units by means of two on-off valves located at the service tank. In the event that the service was shot out, flight could be continued by routing it through a separate line around the tank. Two lines and strainers were used between the service tanks and the power sections to increase engine reliability.

The service tank was pressurized by the vapor pressure of the fuel to 2 psi gage across the tank walls to reduce fuel losses due to boiling. This pressure was maintained by means of a pressure relief valve in the service tank vent system. An automatic pressure release for landing and a manual release for combat operations or emergency were incorporated in the system. The auxiliary tanks were vented into the service tank and were also pressurized.

The lubrication system consisted of a 5½ gallon oil tank including a 1½ gallon expansion space and two 11" diameter oil coolers. The cooler duct inlets were located in the wing fillets and duct exit doors were employed to control the air flow through the coolers.

The engine combustion chambers, turbine sections, and tail pipes were enclosed in a fire resistant chamber of corrosion resistant steel.

Maintenance

Ample access and ease of removal and replacement of components were considered mandatory for this aircraft to provide for a high degree of availability when maintained by small crews on the merchant

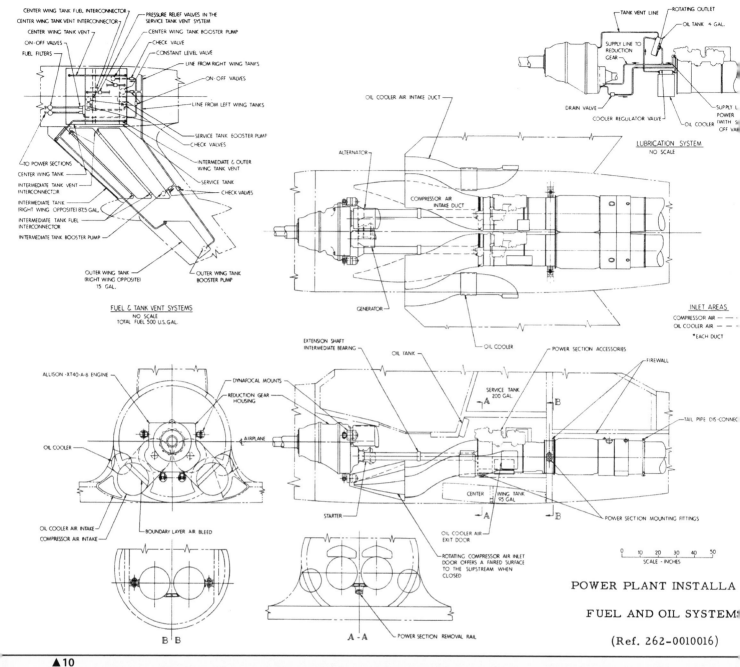

Labels in upper-left diagram (Fuel & Tank Vent Systems):
CENTER WING TANK FUEL INTERCONNECTOR
CENTER WING TANK VENT INTERCONNECTOR
CENTER WING TANK VENT
ON-OFF VALVES
FUEL FILTERS
TO POWER SECTIONS
CENTER WING TANK
INTERMEDIATE TANK VENT INTERCONNECTOR
INTERMEDIATE TANK (RIGHT WING OPPOSITE) 87.5 GAL.
INTERMEDIATE TANK FUEL INTERCONNECTOR
INTERMEDIATE TANK BOOSTER PUMP
OUTER WING TANK (RIGHT WING OPPOSITE) 15 GAL.
PRESSURE RELIEF VALVES IN THE SERVICE TANK VENT SYSTEM
CENTER WING TANK BOOSTER PUMP
CHECK VALVE
CONSTANT LEVEL VALVE
LINE FROM RIGHT WING TANKS
ON-OFF VALVES
LINE FROM LEFT WING TANKS
SERVICE TANK BOOSTER PUMP
CHECK VALVES
INTERMEDIATE & OUTER WING TANK VENT
SERVICE TANK
CHECK VALVES
OUTER WING TANK BOOSTER PUMP

FUEL & TANK VENT SYSTEMS
NO SCALE
TOTAL FUEL 500 U.S. GAL.

Labels in upper-right diagram (Lubrication System):
TANK VENT LINE
ROTATING OUTLET
OIL TANK 4 GAL.
SUPPLY LINE TO REDUCTION GEAR
DRAIN VALVE
COOLER REGULATOR VALVE
OIL COOLER
SUPPLY L... POWER (WITH S... OFF VA...

LUBRICATION SYSTEM
NO SCALE

Labels in middle diagram:
OIL COOLER AIR INTAKE DUCT
ALTERNATOR
COMPRESSOR AIR INTAKE DUCT
GENERATOR
OIL COOLER

INLET AREAS
COMPRESSOR AIR ——
OIL COOLER AIR — —
*EACH DUCT

Labels in lower diagrams:
ALLISON -XT40-A-8 ENGINE
DYNAFOCAL MOUNTS
REDUCTION GEAR HOUSING
AIRPLANE
OIL COOLER
OIL COOLER AIR INTAKE
COMPRESSOR AIR INTAKE
BOUNDARY LAYER AIR BLEED
EXTENSION SHAFT INTERMEDIATE BEARING
OIL TANK
POWER SECTION ACCESSORIES
FIREWALL
SERVICE TANK 200 GAL.
TAIL PIPE DIS-CONNECT
STARTER
CENTER WING TANK 95 GAL.
OIL COOLER AIR EXIT DOOR
ROTATING COMPRESSOR AIR INLET DOOR OFFERS A FAIRED SURFACE TO THE SLIPSTREAM WHEN CLOSED
POWER SECTION MOUNTING FITTINGS
POWER SECTION REMOVAL RAIL

B-B   A-A

0 10 20 30 40 50
SCALE - INCHES

POWER PLANT INSTALLA...
FUEL AND OIL SYSTEM...
(Ref. 262-0010016)

▲10

ship.

The engine reduction gear and dual power section were mounted separately in the fuselage. Access to the aft side of the reduction gear was obtained through the recovery gear compartment which was open when the spike was down. In this area the reduction gear supports and accessories, drive shafts, and radar nose section support were accessible. Release of the radar nose section at this point permitted the removal of the radar nose and exposed the propeller thrust nut for propeller removal. The reduction gear unit was pulled forward out of the fuselage center section.

Removal of the dual power unit was accomplished by separation of the fuselage at the rear wing spar bulkhead. Access doors in the aft fuselage section permitted disconnection of the tail pipe from the engine. Access was provided to quick-disconnects at the fuselage break for tail surface controls and elec-

10) Blueprint showing the installation of the Allison XT-40-A-8 turboprop engine along with the associated fuel and oil systems in the Martin Model 262.

trical lines. The fuselage was separated by removal of five tension bolts. The aft power unit supports were then accessible. The forward power unit support was mounted in a track which permitted the power unit to be withdrawn to the point where the forward support could be grasped for complete removal. Access, without removing the engine, to all accessories, supports, and lines on the forward end of the dual power unit was provided through a large non-structural access door on either side of the fuselage.

Electronic equipment in the upper portion of the aft fuselage section was fully accessible through large, quickly openable doors on the side of the fuselage.

Guns mounted in the under-wing pods were

serviced and removed through large non-structural doors on the sides of the pods. An ammunition box access door was located on the upper surface of the forward end of each pod. Wing gears mounted in the underwing pods and between the guns were accessible through the gear doors on the lower surface of the pod.

Lower surface panels in the wing provided access to the wing fuel cells. Spoiler controls in the wing leading edge were accessible through a door in the leading edge. Controls in the wing above the pod were open to inspection through the wing gear well or could be exposed by removal of the upper cover in this area.

To simplify maintenance and spare parts problems, identical right- and left-hand assemblies were used for the tip fins, the horizontal stabilizers and elevons, the wing spoilers, and wing gears.

▼ 11

Structure & Producibility

Design of the airplane and its tooling were planned to minimize the elapsed time between the experimental program and the delivery of production articles. This was accomplished by incorporating certain production features in the design of the experimental airplane and in the tools used to fabricate these airplanes. The degree to which these production aspects were incorporated was tempered by economic considerations.

The structural design was based on the use of shapes and fabricating methods which were readily adaptable to large scale production. Major produc-

11) **Martin designed the Model 262 to be easily serviced and maintained, with several identical right- and left-hand components to minimize the need for spares.**

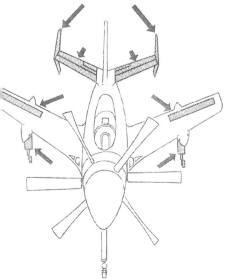

IDENTICAL
RIGHT & LEFT HAND
ASSEMBLIES

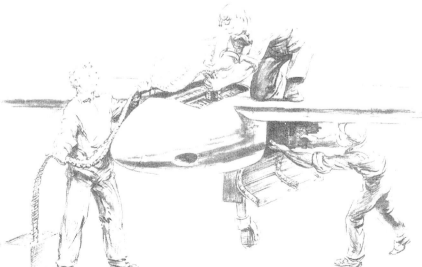

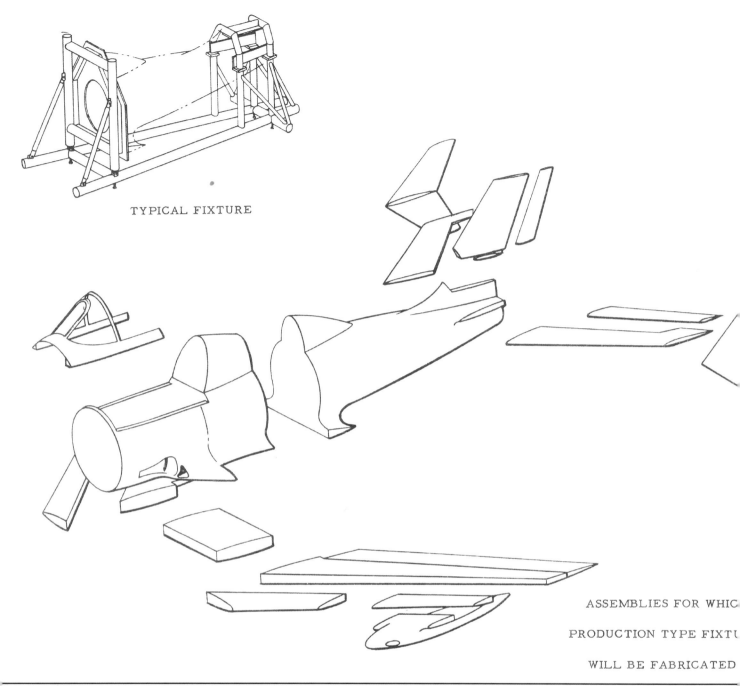

TYPICAL FIXTURE

ASSEMBLIES FOR WHIC

PRODUCTION TYPE FIXTU

WILL BE FABRICATED

▲12

tion splices would have been incorporated in the experimental airplanes. The design would have employed forgings, castings, and extrusions in all applications where they were used in the production airframe except where excessive elapsed procurement time or tooling cost necessitated substitution. When this occurred, the part would have been made to conform as closely as possible to the configurations and physical properties of the production counterpart.

In considering design producibility for this airplane, several salient features were introduced which enabled adaptation of the airplane to high rates of production. The basic cross-sectional shape of the fuselage center section was circular, and for its major portion this assembly was cylindrical. Although the wing fillet altered this shape locally, it permitted the use of radius cut frame tools which were symmetri-

12) Exploded view of the Model 262, which was designed with large scale production in mind.

cal about their centerlines. The cylindrical shaped permitted multiple usage of frame sections between longerons as well as straight lengths for longerons and single curvature forming or rolling of skin and door panels. The fuselage aft section had basic cross sections which were circular, permitting the use of a reduced number of tools with multiple usage for circular frame sections. For the greatest possible extent this portion of the fuselage was made conical with straight line elements for single curvature forming of skin panels and straight longerons.

Prior to engine installation, the fuselage interior presented a clear opening which facilitated assembly of the units. The large fuselage access doors provided for maintenance of the engine and electronics equipment further facilitated this assembly. The pressurized cockpit enclosure area was contained entirely within the fuselage center section. This permitted complete sealing of the pressurized area and subsequent pressure testing of this fuselage section prior to its attachment to other major structural components.

The wing center section between the outer panels was rectangular in planform and of constant section, thereby resulting in straight spar chords, rectangular spar webs, constant length spar stiffeners and single curvature surface covers. The fixed wing and tail surfaces were of the blanket type construction which permitted use of a minimum number of ribs and lent itself to a means of assembly that was not handicapped by the very limited access between the covers of the thin airfoil surfaces.

The wing spoiler aft of the rear spar was made with a flat surface and its ends were cut normal to its length. This eliminated all contour in this surface and

permitted manufacture of identical parts for the right and left wing installations. Identical right and left hand assemblies were also being employed for stabilizers, elevons, tip fins, and wing gears. Thin trailing edge surfaces such as elevons, rudder, fin tips, and tabs were made of metal honey comb construction, metal covered, for greatest economy eliminating numerous detail sheet metal parts.

Splices between the wing center section and outer panel as well as the attachment of fixed tail surfaces to fuselage stubs were of the simplest practical interchangeable design employing a minimum of matching surfaces and attachments. If design considerations permitted, tension type splices would have been employed. The fuselage splice between center and aft section was of the simple tension bolt type employing five tension bolts with intermediate

---

13) Structural diagram of Martin's VTOL turboprop fighter showing the major frames, longerons, spars, etc.

▼ 13

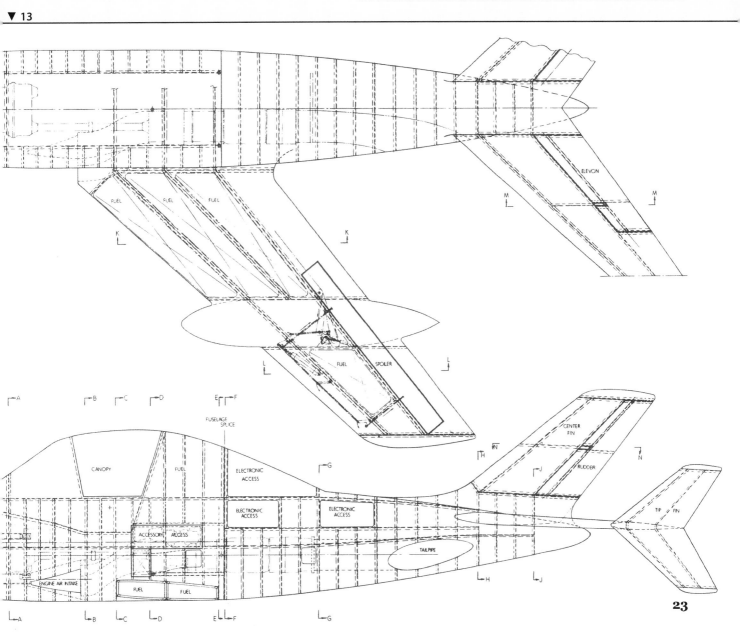

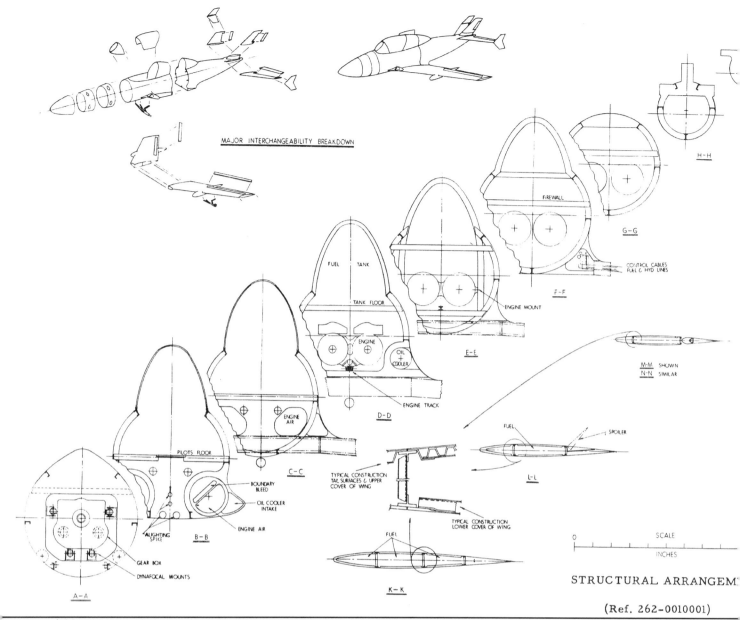

MAJOR INTERCHANGEABILITY BREAKDOWN

H-H

FIREWALL

G-G

CONTROL CABLES
FUEL & HYD LINES

F-F

FUEL   TANK

TANK FLOOR

ENGINE MOUNT

ENGINE

OIL
COOLER

E-E

M-M SHOWN
N-N SIMILAR

ENGINE TRACK

D-D

ENGINE
AIR

FUEL

SPOILER

L-L

PILOTS FLOOR

C-C

TYPICAL CONSTRUCTION
TAIL SURFACES & UPPER
COVER OF WING

BOUNDARY
BLEED

OIL COOLER
INTAKE

TYPICAL CONSTRUCTION
LOWER COVER OF WING

ENGINE AIR

ALIGHTING
SPIKE

B-B

FUEL

SCALE

INCHES

GEAR BOX

DYNAFOCAL MOUNTS

K-K

STRUCTURAL ARRANGEM.

A-A

(Ref. 262-0010001)

▲14

self-engaging studs for shear load transfer.

Major assembly and subassembly tools were of the production type designed with provisions for all locators, drill plates, trim bars, and other refinements required for ultimate production. These assembly tools also contained temporary experimental tooling features such as contour boards, auxiliary locators, etc., to take the place of minor subassembly tools. Tools used to fabricate detail parts and small subassemblies were of the experimental type generally suitable for the manufacture of up to ten airplanes. Wooden or masonite form blocks would have been used in lieu of steel dies to form sheet metal parts.

Modified Arrangements

Three modified arrangements were given serious consideration by Martin during its design studies. The company believed that certain aspects of each of these required further study, both analytically and in the wind tunnel, before deciding on the final configu-

14) Structural arrangement of the Martin Model 262 showing major fuselage cross sections. The basic cross section of the center fuselage was circular, which lowered the cost of producing the aircraft.

ration of the convoy fighter.

The manner in which this airplane was expected to be flown introduced aerodynamic problems which could not be analyzed by conventional and proven methods. Applicable methods of analysis had been evolved during Martin's design studies and were presented in accompanying engineering reports. These methods were derived primarily from theoretical considerations. They had not been proven experimentally since very little experimental data existed.

Martin found that the method of analysis and the evaluation of various aerodynamic effects had a profound influence on the selection of the optimum configuration. Therefore, the company planned to verify their methods of analysis by wind tunnel tests before proceeding with the construction of the

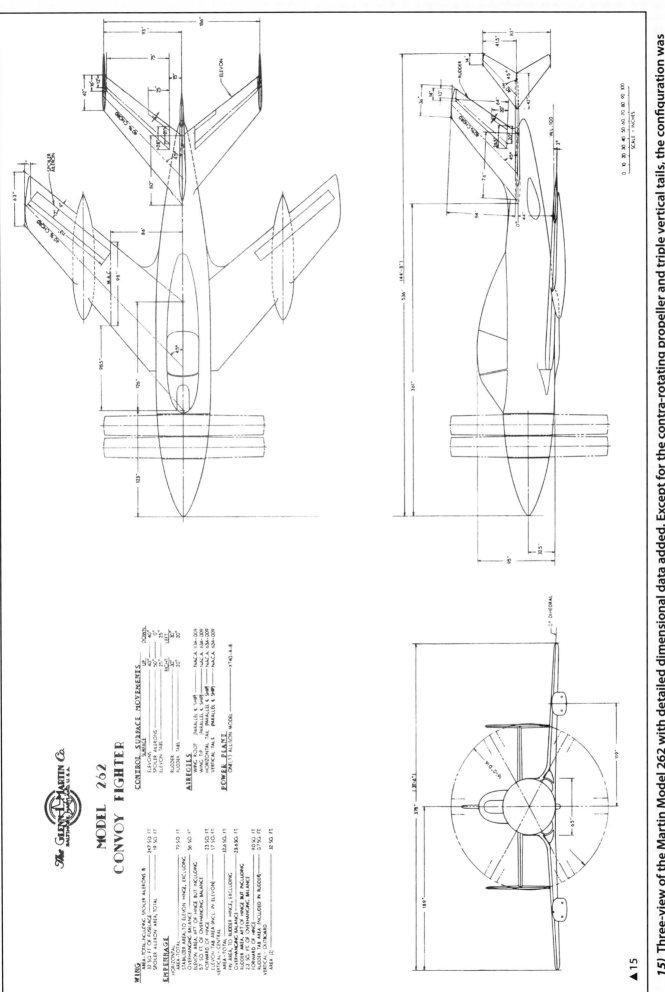

15) Three-view of the Martin Model 262 with detailed dimensional data added. Except for the contra-rotating propeller and triple vertical tails, the configuration was relatively conventional for a fighter of the early 1950s.

25

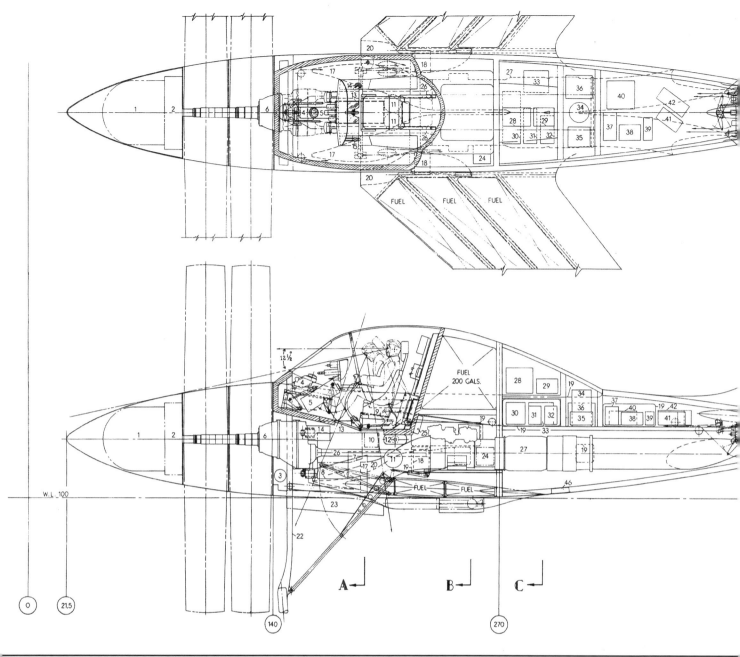

airplane. The modifications which Martin envisaged as possible solutions to the convoy fighter problems involved a different propeller location for each configuration: one mounted the propeller on the nose, the second was centrally located, while the third had the propeller aft in a pusher installation.

General arrangement and inboard profile drawings are shown for two modifications using delta wings. In addition, the swept wing airplane modified to locate a pusher propeller between the wing and the tail is shown.

An alternate propeller gearing arrangement was also included which provided various speeds of propeller operation without a gear shift. This was presented for possible consideration in lieu of a gear shifting arrangement if two propeller speeds became mandatory to meet the propeller's performance requirements.

Modification A—Delta Wing. The delta wing planform offered several distinct advantages in the convoy fighter application. A considerable saving in wing and tail weight was achieved which resulted in increased loiter time and reduced airframe weight. It permitted the elimination of the horizontal tail whose contribution to stability in level flight was comparatively small. Tail buffet problems in high speed flight were eliminated. The ability to perform constant altitude transitions was much improved since very little of the wing was outside of the slipstream. The disadvantages of this planform were the reduction in rate of climb and ceiling due to the lower span and possible reduction in longitudinal control response with no horizontal tail.

The pilot was located immediately behind the propellers in a large canopy. The radar scanner was in the propeller spinner. Engine air was inducted through flush air intakes in the side of the fuselage.

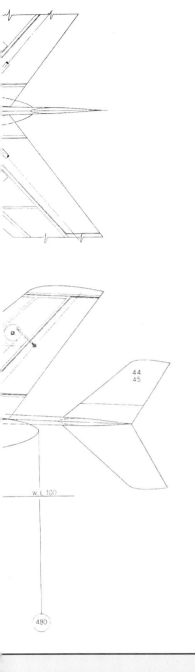

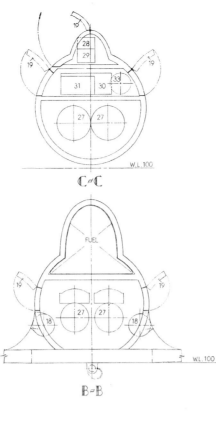

C~C

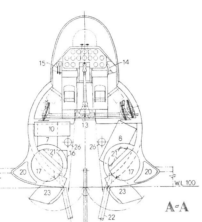

B~B

A~A

1. APQ-42 SCANNER
2. APQ-42 R. F. HEAD
3. OXYGEN BOTTLE
4. MK. 6 SIGHT UNIT
5. APQ-42 SCOPE
6. REDUCTION GEAR HOUSING AND EQUIPMENT
7. LEAD ANGLE COMPUTER
8. AC & DC ELECTRICAL CENTER
9. PILOT'S PIVOTING EJECTION SEAT
10. POWER SUPPLY
11. FIRE EXTINGUISHER TANK
12. CABIN CONDITIONING UNIT
13. PILOT'S FLOOR WINDOW
14. FORMATION STICK
15. POWER CONTROLS
16. FLIGHT DATA COMPUTER
17. ENGINE AIR INTAKE
18. OIL COOLER
19. ACCESS DOOR
20. OIL COOLER INTAKE
21. BOUNDARY AIR BLEED
22. RETRIEVING SPIKE
23. GEAR & ACCESS DOOR
24. BATTERY
25. OIL TANK
26. DRIVE SHAFT
27. DUAL POWER PLANT UNIT (XT40-A-8 ALLISON)
28. APX-6 TRANSPONDER
29. APQ-42 INDICATOR CIRCUITS
30. ARC-27 TRANSCEIVER
31. APQ-42 SERVO AMP.
32. APQ-42 CONVERTER AMP.
33. APQ-42 RADAR CENTRAL
34. APQ-42 MODULATOR
35. INVERTER
36. HYDRAULIC RESERVOIR
37. APQ-42 AC REGULATOR
38. APQ-42 GYRO POWER SUPPLY
39. APQ-42 AMPLIFIER
40. APQ-42 REG. POWER SUPPLY
41. ARR-2A NAV. RADIO
42. APN-22 TRANS. RCVR.
43. APN-22 ANTENNA
44. ARC-27 ANTENNA (RIGHT TAIL FIN)
45. IFF ANTENNA (LEFT TAIL FIN)
46. ARR-2A ANTENNA

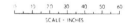

SCALE - INCHES

INBOARD PROFILE

MODEL 262

(Ref. 262-0010004)

16) Inboard profile of the Model 262; note the rotating pilot's seat and ventral window under the cockpit to aid him in "sticking" a landing on the recovery platform with the nose spike.

17) Artist's impression of the Martin Model 262 in flight.

Engine exhaust was aft through the sides of the fuselage. Fuel was carried in the forward part of the wing and in a service tank in the fuselage.

The four 20 mm guns were mounted in bodies of revolution on each wing tip. Their ammunition was carried in spanwise ducts in the wing.

Lateral control was supplied by differential operation of the elevons on the wing trailing edge. Longitudinal control was

▲17

▲18

18) Martin looked at three additional configurations during the development of its convoy fighter proposal. Modification A of the Model 262 was a delta wing design which achieved significant reduction in wing and tail weight, increasing loiter time and reducing overall airframe weight.

19) Modification B was a delta wing design with a centrally located propeller. This reduced the moment arm from the propeller to the center of gravity of the airplane, minimizing the destabilizing effects of the propeller. However, with this layout, the gear box and propeller hub assembly had to be adapted to permit the support of the forward fuselage.

▲19

▲20

20) Modification C had a swept wing planform with the propeller located in the aft fuselage behind the wing and forward of the tail. In this location, the propeller was no longer destabilizing in level flight but contributed to overall stability and enabled a reduction in tail size. Note the prone position of the pilot.

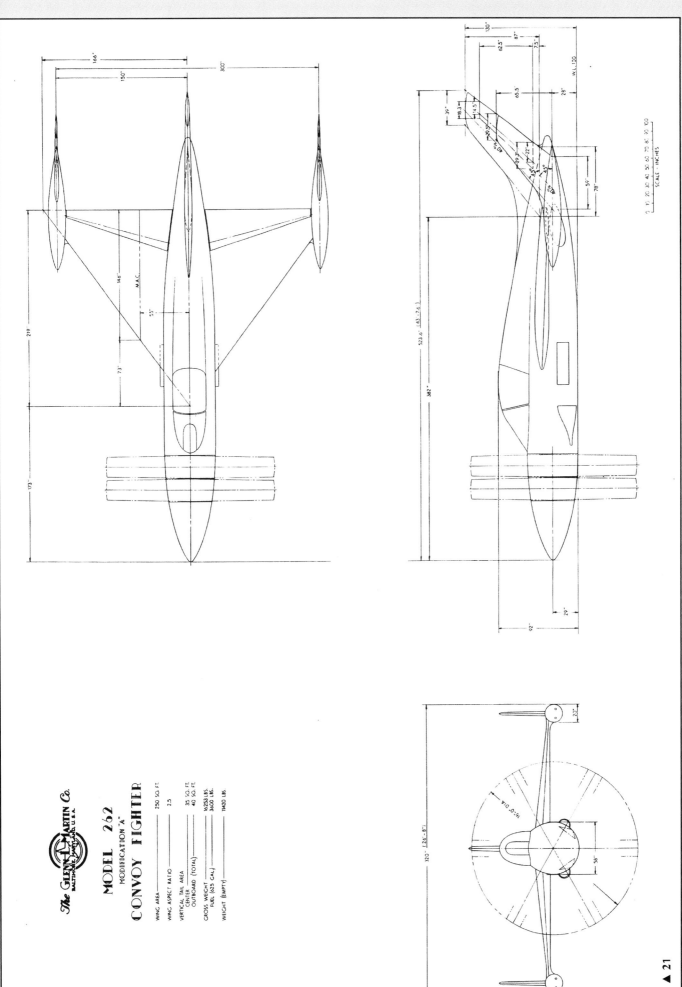

MODEL 262
MODIFICATION "A"
CONVOY FIGHTER

WING AREA	250 SQ. FT.
WING ASPECT RATIO	2.5
VERTICAL TAIL AREA	
CENTER	35 SQ. FT.
OUTBOARD (TOTAL)	40 SQ. FT.
GROSS WEIGHT	16,253 LBS.
FUEL (625 GAL.)	3600 LBS.
WEIGHT (EMPTY)	11420 LBS.

The Glenn L. Martin Co.
BALTIMORE, MARYLAND, U.S.A.

21) Three-view of the Martin Model 262 Modification A delta wing convoy fighter, the primary advantage of which was reduced airframe weight.

▲ 21

29

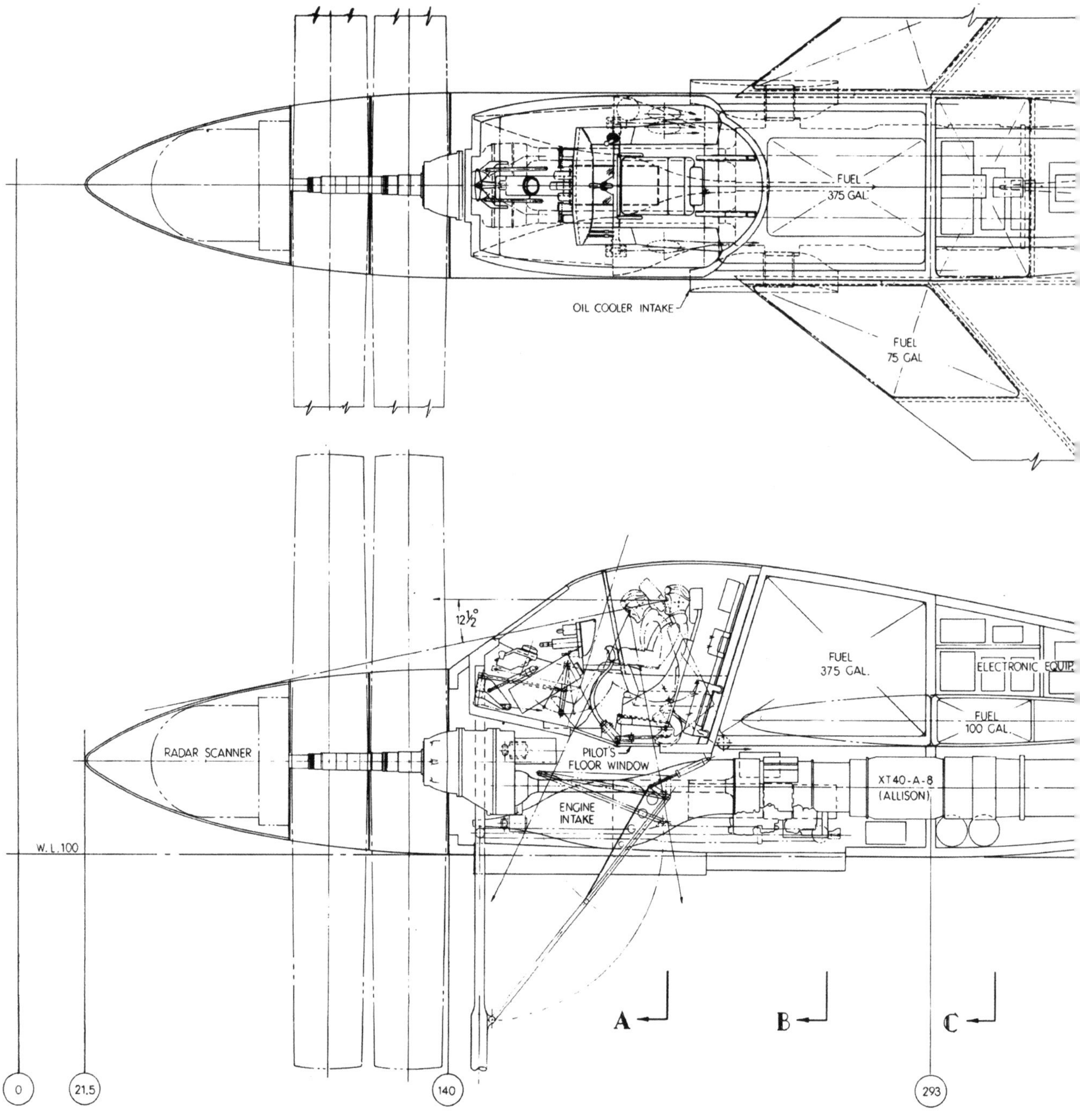
FUEL
375 GAL
OIL COOLER INTAKE
FUEL
75 GAL
12½°
FUEL
375 GAL.
ELECTRONIC EQUIP.
FUEL
100 GAL.
RADAR SCANNER
PILOT'S
FLOOR WINDOW
ENGINE
INTAKE
XT40-A-8
(ALLISON)
W. L. 100
A
B
C
0
21.5
140
293

▲22

through symmetrical displacement of these elevons. Directional control was provided by a rudder on the central vertical surface. The additional vertical surface required for directional stability in horizontal flight was supplied by the fins mounted on the tip bodies which were not in the slipstream.

Modification B—Central Propeller. This modification was envisioned with a delta wing and consequently realized the same advantages and disadvantages as the "A" modification. However, the central propeller location reduced the moment arm from the propeller to the center of gravity of the airplane. The destabilizing effects of the propeller were then minimized. The pilot, the radar and the guns were mounted in the fuselage forward of the propellers. The pilot's forward vision was then unimpaired by the propeller and in an emergency the pilot could be ejected in a capsule rather than in an ejection seat. Increased gun fire accuracy and aerodynamic cleanliness resulted from the installation of the guns and radar in the fuselage nose.

Engine air was taken aboard through intakes in the wing root. Engine exhaust was through the sides of the fuselage in the rear. Fuel was carried in the forward part of the wing and in the fuselage. The control surfaces operated the same as in the "A" modification.

Since this modification required supporting a part of the fuselage forward of the propeller, the gear box and propeller hub assembly had to be adapted to permit this support. Preliminary discussions with the

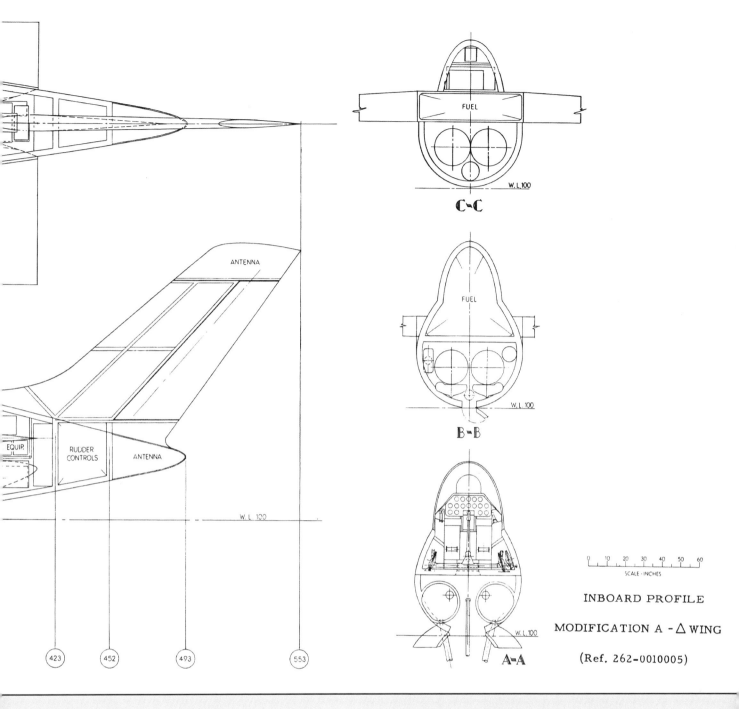

22) Inboard profile of the Modification A delta wing study, a lighter and simpler version of the Model 262.

gear box and propeller manufacturers indicated that this probably could be provided.

Modification C—Pusher Propeller. This modification placed the propeller aft of the center of gravity in a pusher installation. The propeller was then no longer destabilizing in level flight but contributed to the stability with a consequent reduction in required tail size. With the propeller operating behind the wing, 1-P propeller stresses were greatly reduced since the downwash of the wing tended to cause the propeller to act at a small and constant angle of attack throughout the entire speed range. The tails were located behind the propeller in the slipstream to provide control during hovering. Since the wing was ahead of the propeller, the possibility

of a drag increment induced by the slipstream acting over the wing was eliminated. Engine exhaust was through eight louvers equally spaced around the fuselage to allow the exhaust to mix with the free-steam before passing through the propeller disk.

Locating the pilot, radar and guns in the nose provided the same advantages in pilot's vision and armament installation as was found in the "B" modification. With the pilot prone, the large canopy was eliminated, a small frontal area and favorable length-diameter ratio were realized.

The disadvantage of the arrangement was the extra effort which had to be born by the engine and

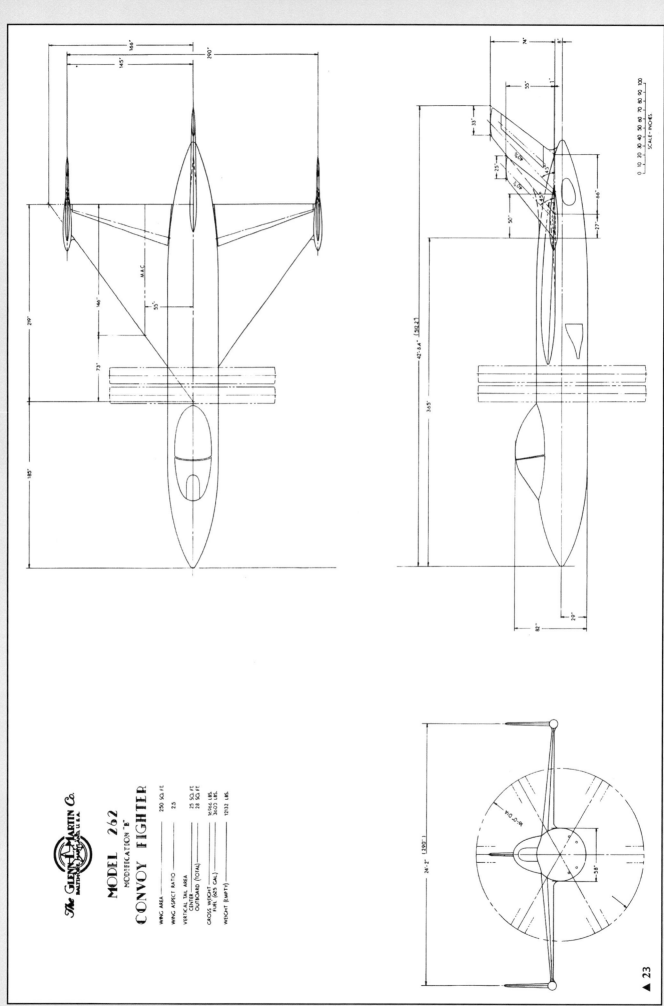

The Glenn L. Martin Co.
BALTIMORE, MARYLAND, U.S.A.

MODEL 262
MODIFICATION "B"

CONVOY FIGHTER

WING AREA	250 SQ. FT
WING ASPECT RATIO	2.5
VERTICAL TAIL AREA	
CENTER	25 SQ. FT.
OUTBOARD (TOTAL)	28 SQ. FT.
GROSS WEIGHT	16,966 LBS.
FUEL (625 GAL.)	3,603 LBS.
WEIGHT (EMPTY)	12,132 LBS.

▲ 23

23) Three-view of the Martin Model 262 Modification B delta wing study with the propeller located mid-fuselage just behind the cockpit and forward of the wing.

propeller manufacturers. The propeller drive shaft had to be move to the exhaust side of the engine. The propeller hub and gear box again had to be capable of accommodating a support structure as in Modification "B"—this time for the tail surfaces.

Alternate Gearing Arrangement. During Martin's studies of the pusher propeller configuration (Modification C), a propeller gearing arrangement compatible with the configuration was investigated. It consisted of a differential ring gear arrangement driving one fixed pitch propeller and one variable pitch propeller in contra-rotation. This arrangement provided a variation in propeller speeds without resorting to a gear shifting arrangement.

Use of the ring gear provided the space through the center of the gear box for airframe structure and control lines. The differential feature split the torque equally between the two contra-rotating propellers and eliminated all rolling trim changes due to power. Their relative speeds were then a function of the blade angle on the variable pitch propeller which was governed by the engine RPM. Thus, for hovering, the variable pitch propeller was made to operate at low blade angles and consequently high RPM. Since the torque was always equally divided between the two propellers, the variable pitch propeller then absorbed most of the engine power output and efficiently converted it to thrust. An increase in the diameter or number of blades may have been required to absorb the power. The large differences in the RPM of the two propellers produced a gyroscopic effect which should have contributed materially to hovering stability.

For the high speed flight regime, the pitch was increased so as to make both propellers turn at comparable (lower) RPM's. Power was then divided about equally between the propellers. The fixed pitch propeller was profiled to produce maximum efficiencies at high speeds. A weight saving would have been realized by having one propeller of fixed pitch.

Although this gear arrangement was conceived for use in the pusher arrangement, it could have also been adapted to the other arrangements.

Wind Tunnel Program

The proposed wind tunnel program was designed to produce sufficient aerodynamic data to develop a successful prototype airplane which would have ultimately led to the optimum convoy fighter configuration.

Aerodynamically, the prototype powered by the Double Mamba engine was almost identical to the convoy fighter which was powered by the Allison XT-40-A-8. However, this difference in power plants caused the placement of the pilot's canopy and the intake ducts to differ in the two. The initial wind tunnel tests would have been aimed at producing a successful prototype and therefore the wind tunnel model configurations would have adhered to the geometry dictated by the installation of the Mamba engine. In this way, an invaluable direct comparison between wind tunnel and flight test data would have been obtained for use in designing the convoy fighter.

Five separate types of wind tunnel tests were proposed. These, in their proper order, were:
1. Isolated propeller tests
2. Low speed (powered) complete model static tests
3. Free flight model tests
4. Engine intake duct tests
5. High speed complete model tests

Modifications to the basic proposal showed promise of leading to a successful design. These could not have been evaluated until quantitative data was available from the wind tunnel. Therefore, the low speed static tests and the free flight tests to have been run on the proposed Model 262 configuration would have been paralleled by a similar series of tests to determine the merit of the modifications. The modification tested in the wind tunnel would have been selected after further analytical studies. The duplication of tests would have ceased as soon as one configuration emerged with superior characteristics. This method of testing was expected to lead to the optimum prototype in the shortest length of time. The various types of tests listed above are described in the following paragraphs.

1. *Isolated propeller tests*—Since the propeller became the prime lifting surface during part of the flight, its basic aerodynamic characteristics were needed just as the characteristics of the wing and tail were needed. Therefore, in addition to the thrust and torque properties, the propeller normal forces would have been obtained for angles of attack between zero and ninety degrees using a wide range of blade angles and advance diameter ratios. Although the propeller for these tests was to have been used later on the prototype wind tunnel models, the scope of the propeller tests would have been made sufficiently broad to encompass power loadings required for the convoy fighter. The data obtained would have provided the information to set correct blade angles and power input for the model tests and also a means of interpreting

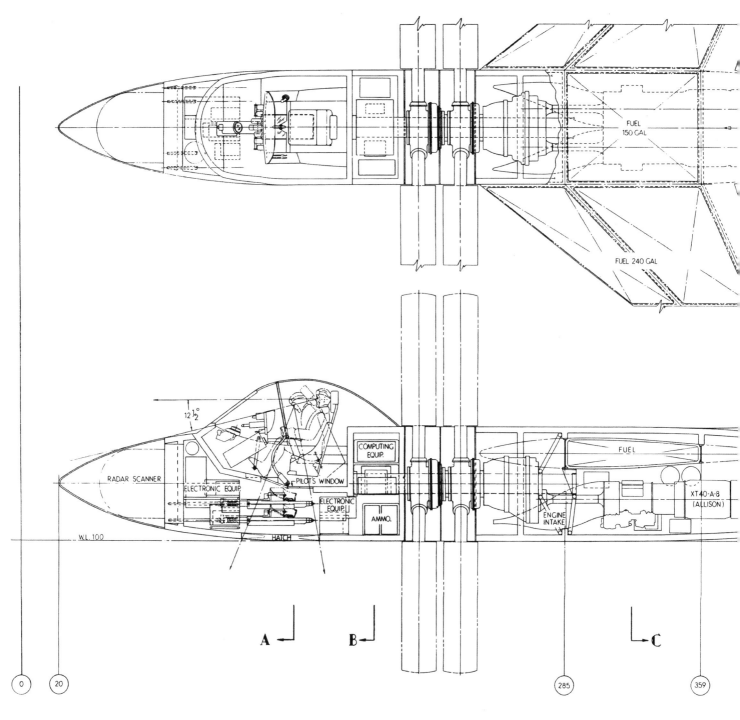

FUEL
150 GAL

FUEL 240 GAL

12 ½°

RADAR SCANNER

ELECTRONIC EQUIP.

PILOTS WINDOW

COMPUTING EQUIP.

FUEL

ELECTRONIC EQUIP.

AMMO.

ENGINE INTAKE

XT40-A-8 (ALLISON)

W.L. 100

HATCH

A

B

C

0   20   285   359

▲24

2. *Low speed tests*—Power off runs were to have been made from zero lift to stall. Tests with power would have been run to cover the high speed, takeoff, transition and hovering phases of flight. A ground board would have been used during some of the takeoff studies. Special emphasis was placed on establishing the optimum wing and tail position relative to the thrust line. Although the prototype configurations would have been tested, power conditions compatible with the requirements of the convoy fighter would have been investigated. In addition to obtaining static stability and the effectiveness of all control surfaces, pressure measurements to establish air loads would have been obtained as well as velocity surveys in the vicinity of the engine intakes.

3. *Free flight tests*—The models would have been dynamically similar to the prototype equipped with remotely controlled surfaces and power plant. Only the hovering and transition near hovering phases of flight would have been investigated on these models. Each model would have first been run in the hovering position and its response to control surface action recorded on film. Next it would have been subjected to horizontal

the effects of power on the airplane components.

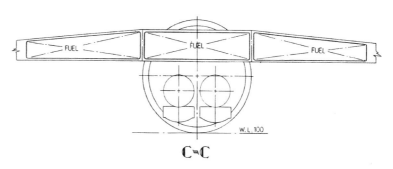

FUEL   FUEL   FUEL

W.L. 100

C-C

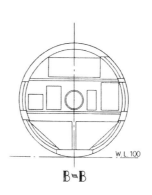

W.L. 100

B-B

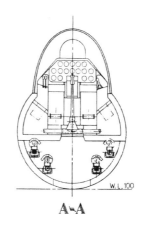

W.L. 100

A-A

W.L. 100

493

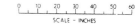

0 10 20 30 40 50 60
SCALE - INCHES

INBOARD PROFILE

MODIFICATION   B

CENTRAL PROPELLER

(Ref. 262-0010006)

winds of various velocities. The model would
have been turned to get the effect of the horizontal wind coming from several quarters to
represent fore and aft drift, lateral drift and
intermediate drifts. Some tests would have
been run close to the ground to investigate
the response to control surface movement in
maneuvers representing the landing condition.

4. *Intake duct tests*—These models would have
been unpowered, fairly large scale models;
one to represent the prototype engine installation and one to represent the convoy
fighter engine installation. Variations in lip
shapes and internal duct lines would have

24) **Inboard profile of the Martin Model 262 Modification
B with a centrally mounted propeller. During an emergency, Martin suggested ejecting the pilot in a capsule rather
than in an ejection seat due to the hazard posed by the
unusual propeller location.**

been provided. The tests would have been
run to obtain the refinement of lip shapes
and internal geometry necessary to obtain a
high critical Mach number entrance and an
optimum duct efficiency for the range of inlet
velocity ratios encountered in flight.

5. *High speed tests*—The high speed of the
prototype airplane was not sufficiently great
to require high speed wind tunnel tests, but

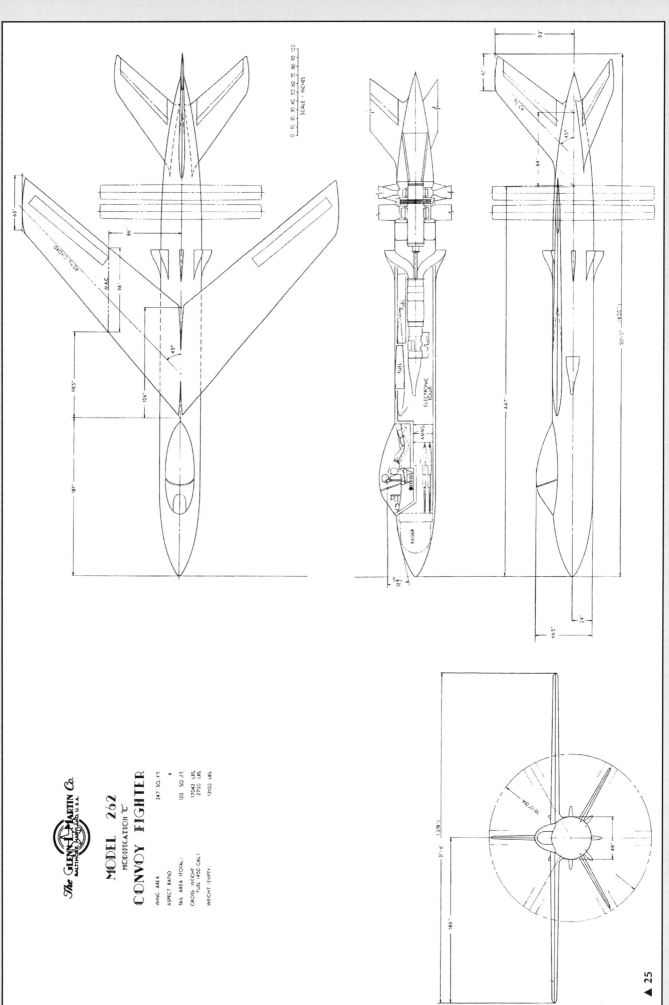

The Glenn L. Martin Co.
BALTIMORE, MARYLAND, U.S.A.

MODEL 262
MODIFICATION "C"
CONVOY FIGHTER

WING AREA   247 SQ.FT.

ASPECT RATIO   4

TAIL AREA (TOTAL)   120 SQ.FT

GROSS WEIGHT   17042 LBS.
     FUEL (450 CAL)   2700 LBS.

WEIGHT (EMPTY)   13100 LBS.

SCALE - INCHES
0 10 20 30 40 50 60 70 80 90 120

25) Three-view of Modification C with the contra-rotating propeller mounted in the aft fuselage; note the 8 engine exhaust louvers just forward of the propeller.

▲ 25

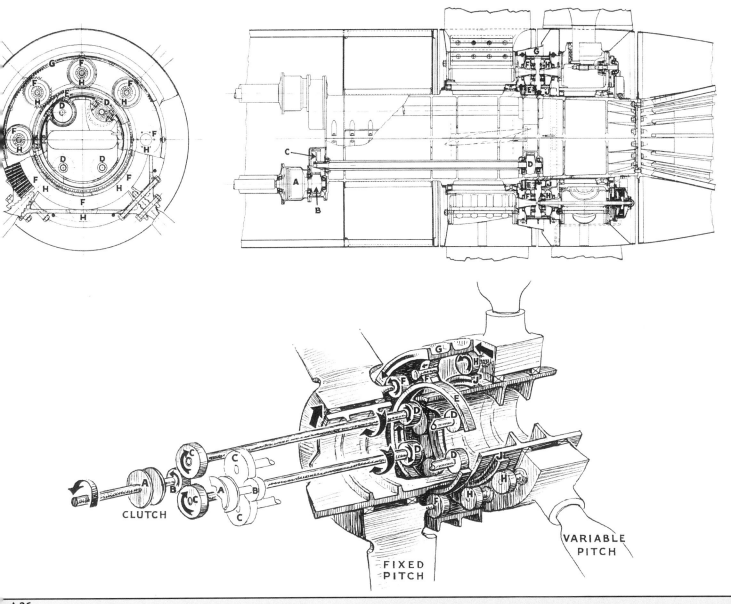

CLUTCH

FIXED PITCH

VARIABLE PITCH

that of the convoy fighter was. The wind tunnel tests would have therefore been performed on a model of the convoy fighter configuration. These tests could have been accomplished directly after sufficient low speed data had been obtained to design the prototype. In the event that the high speed tests showed the need for some redesign, corresponding changes would have been made in the flying prototype design to ensure that it was a true prototype airplane. It was therefore considered necessary to run the high speed tests before proceeding too far with the prototype construction.

Data on performance, stability and control, airloads and pressures adjacent to critical surface junctures would have been obtained by normal wind tunnel techniques. Studies indicated that it would have been unnecessary to equip the high speed model with a power plant. At high speeds the power coefficients were low and it was believed that by providing the model with a windmilling propeller having properly

26) The alternate gear arrangement studied by Martin in connection with Modification C; it consisted of a differential ring gear arrangement driving one fixed pitch propeller and one variable pitch propeller in contra-rotation.

adjusted blade angles, the effects of the propeller on stability could have been adequately reproduced.

Alternate Launch and Recovery

The alternate recovery method described below probably required the least accurate control of the airplane of all those investigated, although the equipment required on the surface ship was rather elaborate. Martin believed that the flight testing of the prototype would have established the direction in which the recovery method development proceeded.

The equipment on the surface ship consisted of a stabilized platform which rolled on curved tracks whose center of curvature coincided with the roll center of the ship. The platform contained sockets

QUALITATIVE COMPARISON

ITEM	MODEL 262 Swept Wing	MODIFICATION A Delta Wing	MODIFICATION B Central Prop.	MODIFICATI⬤ Pusher
Performance				
Maximum Speed	base	comparable	superior	superior
Combat Ceiling	base	inferior	inferior	comparab⬤
Time to Climb to 35,000 Ft.	base	inferior	inferior	comparab⬤
Endurance	base	superior	superior	inferior
Stability				
Hovering	base	comparable	comparable	inferior
Level Flight	base	comparable	superior	superior
Arrangement				
Pilot Vision	base	comparable	superior	superior
Armament Installation	base	comparable	superior	superior
Gear Box Development	base	comparable	inferior	inferior
Weight Empty	base	superior (Lower)	superior (Lower)	inferior (Hig⬤

▲27

which accommodated recovery struts on the aft end of the airplane. Two lengths of flexible steel cable were wound on two winches on the platform.

The airplane was equipped with recovery shock struts on its tail and two lengths of rope which paid out from each wing.

Recovery was accomplished as follows. After making a transition from horizontal to vertical flight, the airplane flew in a hovering attitude in a path which caused the ends of about 75 ft of rope trailing from each wing to be dragged across the after deck of the ship. Deck hands fastened these ropes to the flexible cables located on the stabilized platform. The ropes were then reeled in by the airplane so as to pull the cables up to the airplane and latch them to it. During this operation, the relative vertical motion of the ship and the airplane was taken up by the winches on the platform which automatically reeled the cables in or out so as to keep the cables taut but with a very light load. At the top of one upswing of the ship, the winches were locked. The airplane was then drawn down with the ship as the ship went on its downswing. When the pilot felt this, he applied full power. From then on the cables were kept continually in tension by the excess thrust available from full

27) Table summarizing the pros and cons of the primary Martin Model 262 configuration relative to the alternate Modifications A, B and C.

power operation of the engine and thus there was no longer any relative vertical motion between the ship and the airplane. The airplane was then reeled down onto the platform by the winches on the platform. Suitable devices on the platform then rotated the airplane to the horizontal attitude.

The airplane was launched by standing on its tail on the platform, applying full power, and operating quick-release mechanisms attached to the shock struts.

The cables might have only required use during extremely rough weather. During normal weather conditions, the airplane could have probably been landed on its tail on the platform similar to a helicopter. On shore bases no auxiliary equipment would have been required.

Two cables were used so as to automatically stabilize the airplane in yaw. The cables permitted the airplane to translate sideways but it could not yaw. This kept the thrust line vertical at all times in the plan view of the airplane. In the side view, the cables also tended to stabilize the airplane in pitch but not to the extent that the airplane could not be controlled in pitch by the horizontal tail. The cables were mildly stabilizing in roll when reeled out to long lengths and strongly stabilizing in roll at the shorter lengths.

This recovery method influenced the horizontal tail configuration of the airplane. A three-way tail would have been used to provide for recovering the swept wing airplane on its tail. On the delta wing, modifications to the vertical tail extended above and below the fuselage to accommodate this recovery method.

Model 262P Convoy Fighter Prototype

The prototype for the convoy fighter, designated Model 262P, was an inhabited, flying model (0.766 scale) of the convoy fighter airplane. Dimensional and dynamic similarity to the convoy fighter was

maintained as closely as possible. The prototype was designed in accordance with BuAer Specification OS-122.

The prototype was designed to operate in both the hovering and normal flight regimes. It was aerodynamically similar to the convoy fighter airplane except for the aft location of the pilot and the engine air intakes. These differences were caused by the use of a British Double Mamba engine in place of the XT-40-A-8 engine used in the convoy fighter.

The Model 262P was equipped with a retractable gear for launching and recovery in the hovering attitude which was similar to that of the convoy fighter.

28) Illustration of an alternate recovery method for the Model 262, which involved the aircraft reeling itself in by lengths of cable to the ship, landing on a stabilized platform. This would have required modification of the tail, turning the aircraft into a true tailsitter.

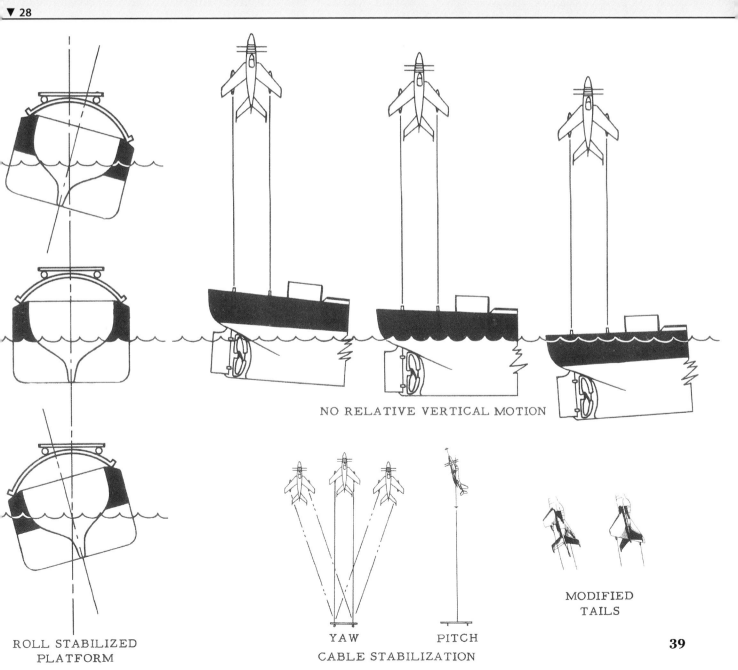

NO RELATIVE VERTICAL MOTION

ROLL STABILIZED
PLATFORM

YAW   PITCH

CABLE STABILIZATION

MODIFIED
TAILS

A truck-mounted recovery platform was designed to accommodate the prototype. A conventional, fixed tricycle landing gear was provided for flight test purposes to permit conventional takeoffs and landings from a runway prior to vertical launching and recovery. Martin considered the temporary installation of a simple split flap to reduce the landing and takeoff speeds during the initial phase of flight testing.

Overall, Martin appears to have put less effort into the design of the Model 262P than the full scale Model 262; it may have determined early on that it was more cost effective for the Navy to build and test a stripped down version of the latter than bother with the three-quarter scale demonstrator.

Cost Proposal

Martin's convoy fighter cost proposal was dated December 1, 1950; it was divided into two parts. Part I included an intensive wind tunnel test and aerodynamic study phase, the design and construction of two prototype scale airplanes, structural proof testing of one of the prototypes, flight testing of the prototypes, and design and furnishing of launching, retrieval and ground handling equipment. Part II included preliminary design data, construction of

29) Artist's impression of the Martin Model 262P convoy fighter prototype, a .766 scale demonstrator powered by a Armstrong Siddeley Double Mamba.

30) Three-view drawing of the compact Model 262P.

a mock-up, additional wind tunnel tests of the full scale configuration, the design and construction of two complete flight articles and one static test article, a complete static test program, a flight test program and the furnishing of launching, retrieval and ground handling equipment.

Based upon the award of a cost plus fixed fee (CPFF) contract having mutually satisfactory provisions, Martin submitted the following quotation for the design and construction of the Model 262 convoy fighter and the prototype airplanes; all amounts are in 1950's dollars. For the scale prototype airplane, the cost was $4,661,159; for the experimental convoy fighter, the cost was $6,399,047. Total for the complete project was $11,060,206. This quote included a 7% fixed fee on estimated costs.

BuAer required contractors to also submit quotes on a fixed price basis. Martin felt that due to the highly experimental nature of the project and the time span involved, that protection against abnormal

The Glenn L. Martin Co.
BALTIMORE, MARYLAND, U.S.A.

MODEL 262P
CONVOY FIGHTER
PROTOTYPE

WING
AREA - TOTAL INCLUDING SPOILER AILERONS 8 ———— 145 SQ. FT.
SQ. FT. OF FUSELAGE
SPOILER AILERON AREA, TOTAL ———— 13 SQ. FT.

EMPENNAGE
HORIZONTAL
AREA - TOTAL ———— 40.5 SQ. FT.
STABILIZER AREA, TO ELEVON HINGE, EXCLUDING
OVERHANGING BALANCE ———— 33.5 SQ. FT.
ELEVON AREA AFT OF HINGE BUT INCLUDING
3.5 SQ. FT. OF OVERHANGING BALANCE
FORWARD OF HINGE ———— 13 SQ. FT.
ELEVON TAB AREA (INCLUDED IN ELEVON) ———— 1 SQ. FT.
VERTICAL - CENTRAL
AREA - TOTAL ———— 19 SQ. FT.
FIN AREA, TO RUDDER HINGE, EXCLUDING
OVERHANGING BALANCE ———— 13.8 SQ. FT.
RUDDER AREA, AFT OF HINGE BUT INCLUDING
1.3 SQ. FT. OF OVERHANGING BALANCE
FORWARD OF HINGE ———— 5.2 SQ. FT.
RUDDER TAB AREA (INCLUDED IN RUDDER) ———— 0.4 SQ. FT.
VERTICAL - OUTBOARD
AREA '2 ———— 19 SQ. FT.

CONTROL SURFACE MOVEMENTS

SURFACE	UP	DOWN
ELEVONS	40°	40°
SPOILER AILERONS	50°	0°
ELEVON TABS	25°	25°

	RIGHT	LEFT
RUDDER	30°	30°
RUDDER TABS	20°	20°

AIRFOILS
WING ROOT ———— PARALLEL ⊄ SHIP ———— N.A.C.A. 63A-009
WING TIP ———— PARALLEL ⊄ SHIP ———— N.A.C.A. 63A-009
HORIZONTAL TAIL ———— PARALLEL ⊄ SHIP ———— N.A.C.A. 63A-00
VERTICAL TAILS ———— PARALLEL ⊄ SHIP ———— N.A.C.A. 63A-00

POWER PLANT
ONE (1) ARMSTRONG SIDDELEY ———— DOUBLE MAMBA

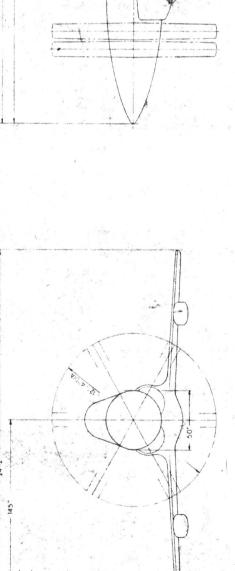

The Glenn L. Martin Co. Baltimore, Md., U.S.A.
MODEL 262P
GENERAL ARRANGEMENT
DWG. NUMBER 262-001G001
PROTOTYPE

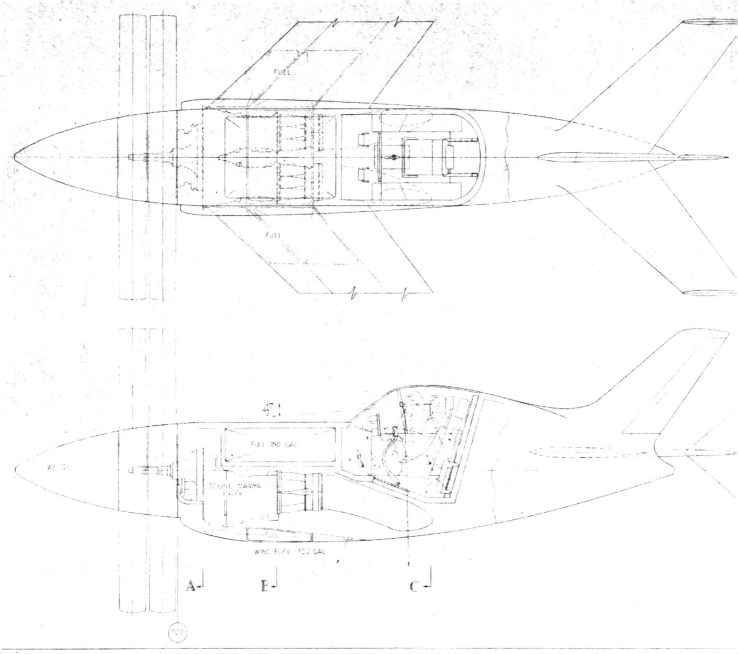

difficulties and rising costs of labor and materiel had to be included in a fixed price quotation. Accordingly, an additional amount was added on a percentage basis to the aforementioned estimated costs to arrive at a fixed price quotation. For the scale prototype airplane, the fixed price cost was $5,693,405; for the experimental convoy fighter, the fixed price cost was $7,808,933. Total for the complete project was $13,502,338 on a fixed price basis.

The above quotations included the following considerations:

1. A very intensive analytical and wind tunnel program, aimed at solving the aerodynamic problems associated with the development of an optimum configuration was planned. Martin assumed that the high speed tunnel tests would be run in a government tunnel at government expense.

2. The estimate included funds for the develop-ment and complete flight testing of a reliable control system for automatically controlling the convoy fighter during level, transitional and hovering flight. This was considered important to the tactical utilization of the aircraft. Although maximum use of existing autopilot components was contemplated, the unusual flight attitudes in which this airplane operated required special sensing equipment.

3. The above prices included all services and data requested by BuAer with one exception to specification SR-38. With regard to the spin requirements, Martin considered that due to the unconventional characteristics of this airplane and its ability to maintain hovering flight, the spin demonstration re-quirements were considered too extreme. In lieu of complying with these requirements,

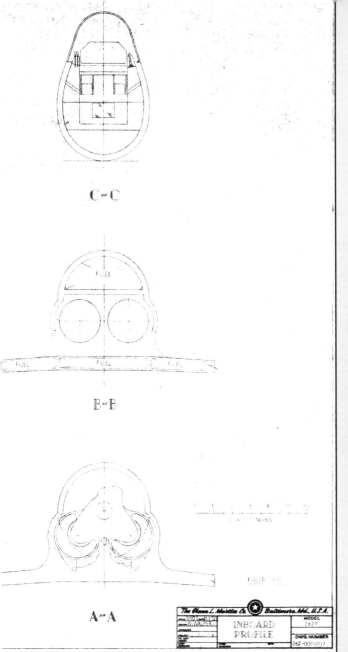

C~C

B~B

A~A

The Glenn L. Martin Co. Baltimore, Md., U.S.A.

INBOARD PROFILE

MODEL
262P

DWG. NUMBER
262-0010007

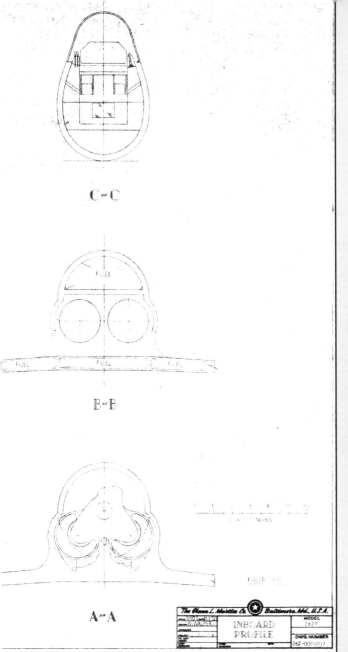

31) Inboard profile of the Martin Model 262P, which was aerodynamically similar to the full scale convoy fighter, except for the location of the pilot and air intakes.

6. The cost of the first complete flight article included basic tooling; the major assembly and major subassembly tooling would have been of the production type.

Martin had evolved a completely automatic blind landing system for recovery of the aircraft when the visibility was down as low as 75 ft. The total estimated cost plus fixed fee to design and furnish a completely automatic blind landing system for the convoy fighter was $674,421. This cost was in addition to that quoted above since such a system was not included in the original requirements.

Martin estimated that the first flight of the prototype would occur 20 months after the authority to proceed was received; the first flight of the first experimental convoy fighter was estimated to occur 18 months after the authority to proceed was received. Although a prototype could have been built and flown in less time than quoted above, Martin felt that detail design and construction should not have begun until sufficient wind tunnel tests and aerodynamic studies had been accomplished to arrive at an optimum configuration. Approximately 8 months were required to accomplish this.

After a review of the total program as proposed, Martin concluded that careful consideration should be given to eliminating the construction of the two scale prototype models and proceeding directly to a full scale article powered by a T-40-6 production engine rated at 5,500 ESHP. This power was sufficient to provide 5 ft/sec² acceleration during the takeoff and transition at a takeoff weight of approximately 13,800 lbs. The weight of the full scale prototype could have been held to this figure by omitting the armament, tactical electronic equipment and some fuel until such time as the 7,500 hp T-40 engine became available. This takeoff weight allowed sufficient fuel on board the airplane to permit flight testing. Since Martin's proposed design was based on the use of a single speed gearbox for the propeller, no gear box availability problems were anticipated. Martin estimated that the time span for the development of the convoy fighter could have been reduced by approximately 14 months and the cost to a total of about $8,000,000 for the entire program if the scale prototypes were eliminated. The company appreciated that there may have been other considerations dictating the use of the prototype scale models of which it was not aware; however, if the alternate plan suggested had merit, a quotation on this basis would have

Martin proposed investigation of the spin characteristics within the limits considered to be safe and practical as indicated by wind tunnel model spin tests and flight handling characteristics.

4. A launch and recovery platform would have been furnished for the prototype and the convoy fighter. The prototype platform would have been mounted on a suitable trailer to facilitate ground handling. The convoy fighter platform would have been suitable for mounting on a trailer or on a ship.

5. Included in the price of the static test article was the cost of an engine test stand for the Mamba engine suitable for checking engine operation, propeller and controls in horizontal and vertical positions. An operable engine test stand was also included in the cost of the first complete flight article.

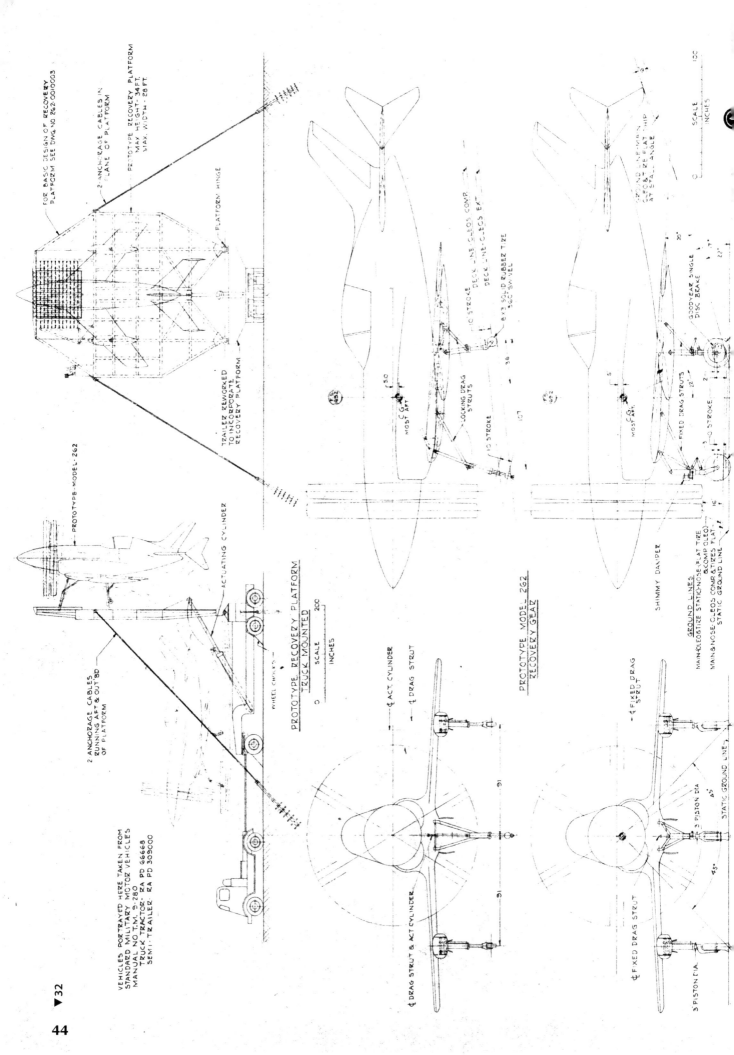

PROTOTYPE RECOVERY PLATFORM
TRUCK MOUNTED

PROTOTYPE MODEL 262
RECOVERY GEAR

SCALE
0   200
INCHES

SCALE
0   100
INCHES

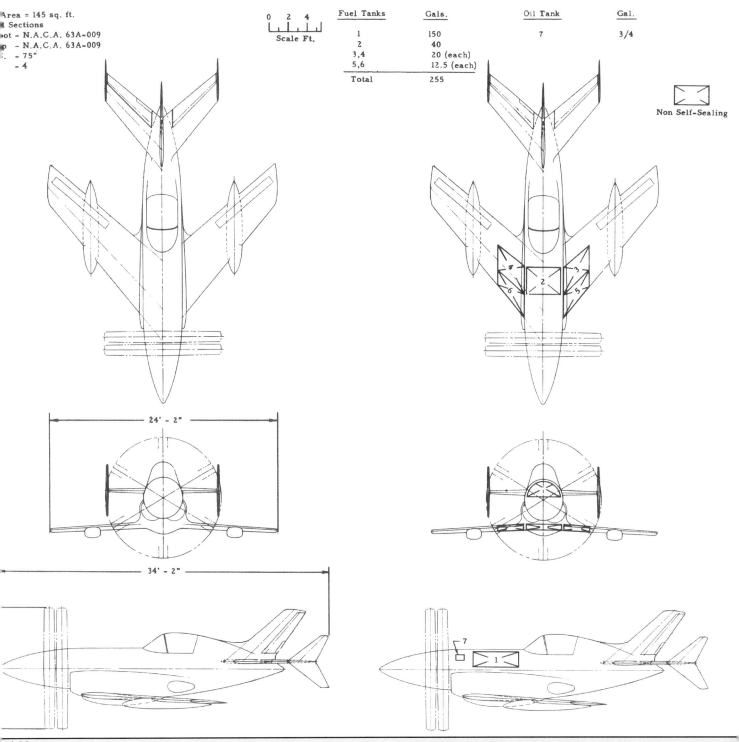

Scale Ft.

0 2 4

Fuel Tanks	Gals.	Oil Tank	Gal.
1	150	7	3/4
2	40		
3,4	20 (each)		
5,6	12.5 (each)		
Total	255		

Non Self-Sealing

24' - 2"

34' - 2"

▲33

been submitted upon request from the government. BuAer would ultimately agree to the elimination of the smaller prototype airplane, but did not award a contract to Martin for reasons discussed in the next section.

Martin definitely preferred a CPFF contract for this type of project, particularly when it was phased and extended over a multi-year period. It requested that any contract resulting from the proposal included provisions for partial payments to the maximum allowable by regulation and for passage of title to the government at the time of the first such payment.

The company claimed that it had the type of personnel and broad experience required to success-

32) Blueprint showing the truck-mounted recovery platform designed to accommodate the Model 262P as well as the auxiliary fixed tricycle landing gear used for flight test purposes, permitting conventional takeoffs and landings from a runway.

33) General arrangement drawings of the Model 262P taken from the Standard Aircraft Characteristics charts prepared for the type; the drawing on the right shows the location of the fuel and oil tanks.

fully develop the proposed convoy fighter and was intensely interested in undertaking the project.

MISSION AND DESCRIPTION

This airplane is an inhabited, flyable model (0.766 scale) of the convoy fighter airplane. Dimensional & dynamic similarity to the convoy fighter are maintained as closely as practicable. The airplane is designed for vertical unassisted take-off from and landing on a vertically positioned platform. It is capable of high performance at altitudes up to approximately 38000 feet.

The Martin Model 262P is a swept wing airplane powered by a British Double Mamba gas turbine engine driving six bladed, 12'-4", contra-rotating propellers. It carries a single pilot and is equipped with an ejection seat. Automatic control devices are provided to assist the pilot. The airplane is designed to serve as a flying scale model from which flight test data may be obtained to assist in the development of the convoy fighter airplane.

WEIGHTS

Loading	Gross Wt.	L.F.
Empty	6559 E	--
Basic	6610 E	--
Design	7735 E(a)	7.5
Flight	7735 E(a)	7.5
Max.T.O.	8348 E(b)	--
Max.Land.	7429 E(c)	--

NOTES:
(a) T.O. less 40% fuel.
(b) Limited by des.reqm't.
(c) T.O. less 60% fuel.

FUEL AND OIL

Max.Gals.	No.Tanks	Loc.
150	1	Fuse.
105	5	Wing

Spec.MIL-F-5616 (JP-1)

OIL

Cap. 3/4 Gals. - 1 Tank
Spec. D. Eng. R.D. 2479

POWER PLANT

No. & Model - Double Mamba III

Mfr. - Armstrong Siddeley Motors Limited
Reduction Gear (Ratio) .1067:1
No Blades/Prop.Dia. 6/12 ft. 4 in.
Prop.Blade Des. - Supersonic, Activity Factor 135 to 150.

RATINGS

	RPM	Prop..Shaft H.P.
T.O.	15000	2600
N.R.P.	14500	2060

	Jet Thrust lbs.	Fuel Cons. lbs./hr.
T.O.	810	1945
N.R.P.	710	1650

ORDNANCE

NONE

DIMENSIONS

Wing Area   145 sq. ft.
Wing Span   24 ft. 2 in.
Wing M.A.C. 75 in.
Max.Airplane Length - 34 ft. 2 in.
Max. Airplane Height - 12 ft. 4 in.

ELECTRONICS

AN/ARC-27   UHF
AN/APN-1   Radio Altimeter

PERFORMANCE SUMMARY

LOADING CONDITION		(1) BASIC
TAKE-OFF WEIGHT	lbs.	8348
Fuel	lbs.	1532
Wing/Power Loading (A)lbs/sq.ft;lbs./bhp.		57.6/2.85
Stall Speed--Power off	kn.	124
Stall Speed--Power off - No Fuel	kn.	112
Stall Speed--Power on	kn.	0
Maximum Speed/Alt (B)	kn./ft.	458/22,000
Take-off Transition Acc.,Min.	ft/sec^2	5.2
Rate of Climb -- Sea Level (B)	ft/min.	7200
Service Ceiling (B)	ft.	38,100
Time-to-climb to 35000 ft. from standstill (B)	min.	13.4
Endurance (A)	min.	45
LOADING CONDITION		(2) COMBAT
GROSS WEIGHT	lbs.	7735
Engine Power		Normal
Fuel (60% Take-Off Fuel)	lbs.	919
Max. speed at sea level	kn.	443
Max. speed/Alt.	kn./ft.	463/22,000
Combat speed/Alt.	kn./ft.	460/35,000
Rate of climb SL	ft/min.	7970
Ceiling for 500 fpm R/C	ft.	37,800

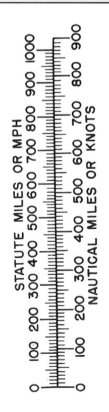

NOTES

(A) 2925 Equivalent Static T.O. Shaft Horsepower.
(B) Normal BHP

(For Continuation of Notes See Page 6)

Why Martin Lost

Based on surviving BuAer notes, I believe the key factor in determining the outcome of the convoy fighter competition was weight. Martin's estimated takeoff gross weight for the Model 262 was 16,890 lbs. BuAer disagreed with this figure, estimating it to be 17,453 lbs, which of course reduced the estimated performance figures of the Model 262. The eventual winners of the competition, Convair and Lockheed, were the lightest of the proposals submitted, with the former being the least heavy of the five contenders. That being said, all of the companies underestimated the takeoff gross weight of their designs to a greater or lesser extent according to BuAer.

Martin seemed to be hedging its bets in their convoy fighter proposal. By presenting three other completely different layouts (Modifications A, B and C), it may have appeared that the company lacked confidence in its basic Model 262 configuration. The alternate recovery scheme shown on p. 39 seems to suggest uncertainty with the main recovery method shown earlier in their brochure. The company's suggestion to engage in extensive research and wind tunnel testing before settling on a final configuration may have run counter to BuAer's expectations; the aircraft ultimately built by Convair and Lockheed were fairly close to their original proposals.

It's also worth noting that the Martin Model 262 was the only swept wing aircraft entered into the competition; the other contractors' proposals were all deltas or straight wing designs. The Model 262 was also not a true tailsitter, hanging instead from a vertical platform; this may not have been BuAer's preference. Whether these factors influenced the Navy's decision will not be known until more documentation emerges.

34-35) Standard Aircraft Characteristics charts for the Martin Model 262P presenting the physical and performance figures for the proposed aircraft.

36) A speculative color profile of the sleek and sharklike Model 262P in an overall Glossy Sea Blue scheme.

37) A photo of the Glenn L. Martin Company of Baltimore, Maryland circa 1950.

▲37

CPSIA information can be obtained at www.ICGtesting.com
Printed in the USA
LVIW01n1059020517
532924LV00006BA/178